Growing up in Sparta

Growing up in Sparta

And Other Adventures

Larry Buege

Gastropod Publishing
126 Ridgewood Dr.
Marquette, Michigan 49855

Other books by Larry Buege

Bear Creek (Humorous)
Miracle In Cade County (Mystery/Love Story)
Cold Turkey (Political Satire)
Super Mensa (Techno-Thriller)
William Goodman: Civil War Horsesoldier

Native American Series:
Chogan and the Gray Wolf
Chogan and the White Feather
Chogan and the Sioux Warrior
Chogan and the Winnebago Merchant

Published by Gastropod Publishing, Marquette, Michigan
Copyright © 2022 by Larry Buege

Library of Congress Control Number: 2021921788

ISBN: 979-8-9851851-5-7

Dedication

To my great, great grandchildren. I hope you will one day discover this biography in an attic and think I lived an interesting life.

Preface to Second Addition

Fiction writers are professional liars. If we write something that is not true, no one cares. Hey, this is fiction. But people expect works of non-fiction to be factual and accurately portrayed. Some readers cheerfully pointed out errors in *Growing Up In Sparta and Other Adventures* (Thank you). Some of these errors were minor, others were more egregious. They have all been corrected in the second edition.

Most of the criticism was not about what was in the biography, but what was left out. It is impossible to document decades of growing up between the covers of one book. As a compromise, I did add new material. There is a section describing S & H Green stamps as well as hitchhiking as a common mode of transportation. Another section follows the evolution of tipping wait staff. Younger people will find this difficult to believe, but tips were not the norm and were given to reward exemplary service. There is an entire chapter devoted to Christmas shopping in Grand Rapids and summer visits to the Ramona Amusement Park.

My target audience was and still is my grandchildren and their grandchildren. This may not be of interest to Sparta readers, but I spent fifteen years in Michigan's only ultra-maximum security prison. (Spoiler Alert: I was an employee.) This section was expanded to include photos of the 1981 riot. There is also a how-to segment explaining how to make a functional pistol from toilet paper, match heads, and a battery casing.

This autobiography was my first experience with incorporating black and white photos, and it appeared to work well. In the second edition there are twenty-seven new photos and eighteen additional pages.

I am not the only person with an interesting life. I hope this biography will inspire others to place their adventures on paper. Your grandchildren will thank you for your effort.

Preface

Many people may question the need for an autobiography by a common man of neither fame nor fortune. The author has accomplished nothing worthy of ink in a history book. The accounts of those who did alter the course of history justly deserve the recognition they receive, but those same accounts lack detail about the soil from which those celebrated personalities sprouted. To fully understand our history we must understand the lifestyles, activities, and hardships facing the common citizen. Ordinary people are essential to our understanding of our history.

Although the title is *Growing up in Sparta*, it could have been *Growing up in Small Town, USA*. The citizens of Sparta may think their town is unique and it is, but Sparta shares similarities and virtues with other small towns across America. Free range children, one-room schoolhouses, and small-town movie theaters were the norm in the '50s and '60s. The author tried to emphasize the culture of the period and minimize his own involvement, but it was necessary to include some exploits to prove that kids will be kids. When given the opportunity, they will make dumb and sometimes dangerous decisions, yet they survived.

The reader may wonder about the inclusion of the Vietnam War and post-war America. It was assumed that any healthy male graduating from Sparta High School in the 1960s would spend a year in Vietnam. The author was no exception. Consistent with the first half of the biography, the author was not a remarkable soldier. He received no Purple Hearts or Bronze Stars. The author's experiences were different, yet similar to the experiences of the hundreds of thousands of men who served in Vietnam.

This biography will not be a best seller. It cannot compete with the simple life of Anne Frank, but its value will increase with time like an aging wine. The author's generation will die off, and there will no longer be memories, only the written word. Then when the author's great, great, grandson or granddaughter discovers a copy among the junk in some attic, it will be priceless.

Contents

–1–
Grandparents

I know little of my maternal grandparents. Elizabeth Louise Reeves died in 1940, six years prior to my birth. Her husband, Stanley Victor Morrill, died in 1954 when I was eight years old. Since he lived with his son in Benton Harbor, I only saw him during brief visits. I remember him as kind and gentle man with a bushy mustache. He tried his hand at farming, but according to my mother he was not a good farmer. He was good with his hands and left us with several wooden heirlooms

My paternal grandparents were born in 1885 and were much younger than my other grandparents. I knew them throughout my teenage years. Alma Miller and Arthur Buege were born in the German-American farming community of Salem Township, located in Allegan County, Michigan. Alma left school after the eighth grade to work on the farm, which was normal for girls at the turn of the century. Eighth grade was as advanced as girls were expected to progress in their education. Only six percent of the population graduated from high school, and they were mostly boys.

Arthur Buege was one of two sons born to a well-to-do first generation German-American farmer. Both Arthur and his brother, Norman, graduated from high school. Norman went on to become a dentist, but died at an early age from tuberculosis.

Arthur Buege with his thirty-three students

Arthur taught school in a one-room schoolhouse. This was a common expectation for high school graduates. Since many of his students spoke only German, he taught classes in both English and German.

Arthur's father died one year after Norman died. Since Arthur was busy teaching school, he needed help on the farm. He hired a Swiss immigrant by the name of Fritz Buhler. Fritz later married Arthur's sister Lidia.

In 1914 Arthur decided he wanted to be a minister, but two years of seminary did not come cheaply. Arthur sold his portion of the farm to Fritz in a land contract. Fritz would send him money during Arthur's two years of seminary. There was also a gentleman's agreement that Fritz would provide a small parcel on which Arthur could build his retirement home. Arthur never retired on the old farm, but Fritz donated cherry lumber for the interior of Arthur's retirement home in Sparta.

I really didn't get to know my paternal grandparents until my grandfather retired from the Methodist Church in Lawrence, Michigan in 1949. Since their daughter, Mildred (Buege) Tanner, and my father lived in Sparta, Michigan, they decided to retire to that community.

I soon discovered they brought with them some of their 19th century pioneer spirit. They purchased a large hillside lot on Harper Drive. The back of the lot sloped steeply down to a cow pasture, owned by Ostman's Dairy Farm.

They owned a lot but had no place to stay. Winter was fast approaching. There was insufficient time to build a house, but there was time to build a one-stall garage. They completed the simple block structure just before the winter snow arrived. They used a wood stove for cooking and heat. A metal exhaust pipe with elbow carried smoke and fumes through the wall to a masonry chimney. The "restroom" was out back under a large elm tree. My grandmother would later plant a flower garden in the area. Flowers over the old outhouse always grew taller than the rest of the flowers. I was three going on four and remember little of the home in a garage, but I do remember the outhouse. It was scary at night. My grandparents felt no shame in such a humble dwelling. My mother said they continued to entertain guests. If the need were to arise, they had a flashlight to guide their guests toward the facilities.

I often wondered where my grandfather obtained his building skills. It is not a skill often taught in seminary other than *you should build your house on rock, not sand*. Guess what? His house was built on sand. During my research I discovered that Arthur's father was a skilled craftsman. Frank Buege, and Arthur's uncle, Charles Raab, built their church in Salem. Arthur was just a teenager at the time and dating Alma. He was assigned the task of making cement blocks by hand. He carved his name and Alma's name on each block. (This was not on the exposed surface.) I am sure he learned many other building skills from his father.

When spring arrived, it was time to build a real home. Arthur hired a bull dozer to dig the basement, but the rest he did on his own. It was my job to play on the large pile of sand excavated from the site.

After the foundation was set, it was time to lay the concrete blocks. Fortunately, they no longer had to be made by hand. Arthur didn't have a fancy motorized cement mixer to make his mortar. Instead he used a handmade trough and a hoe for mixing the cement and gravel. Sometimes he allowed me to mix the cement and gravel prior to adding water. The mixing was always finished by an adult. Perhaps they didn't trust a four year old.

According to my brother, Jack, the sand around the basement blocks caved in, knocking over the wall. My cousin, Bill Tanner, said this happened twice. Anger is not a constructive emotion, and the Rev. Arthur Buege was constructing a home. He dusted himself off and without further utterance began removing the damaged blocks. He dug out the offending sand by hand. Fortunately, the basement floor was still sand.

At that time my grandparents had a neighbor by the name of Mr. Siegel. He was a devout atheist and proud of it. He had a vocabulary of four-letter words that would be the envy of any sailor. After watching the wall fail repeatedly and watching Arthur repeatedly start over without so much as a "Why me, Lord?" Mr. Siegel proclaimed, "That is one damn fine man!"

A little more needs to be said about Mr. Siegel. Not only was he an atheist with a potty mouth, he was also perpetually grumpy—and hated kids. My older brother and I fit that last description. We were constantly admonished to stay away from his yard. One day we were playing ball, and the ball accidentally rolled into his yard. He was watering his flowers with a hose at the time. He immediately swung the hose around to spray the ball. We quickly scampered over to retrieve the ball but got soaked for our effort.

One would think such a grumpy atheist and a retired pastor would not be good neighbors, but such was not the case. My grandmother was always bringing over cookies or pecan rolls or produce from their garden. Whether Mr. Siegel liked it or not, he was one of God's children and would be treated accordingly. That was how my grandparents were. During the Great Depression, no hobo who knocked on their door ever left hungry.

Their retirement home was built on a plateau, but their lot sloped down into a field next to Nash Creek. This area is where they decided to plant their garden. They called it a garden, but in reality it was a small farm. They hired someone from the neighboring Ostman farm to plow the soil—the garden was too big to turn over by hand. Both grandparents grew up on farms, so farming was in their blood. They thought nothing of toiling away the summer in their beloved garden. They planted two rows of sweet corn every two weeks until they had six or eight long rows. The corn would then ripen throughout the summer.

Once the corn was ripe we were invited over for a corn feast. I don't remember if there was anything else on the menu, but there was a huge platter of freshly boiled sweet corn. There is no sweeter corn than the corn that is picked after the pot of water begins to boil. They canned some of the corn, but they still grew more corn than they could eat or can. The rest of the corn was for sharing. They took pride in offering some of their bounty to others. I am sure Mr. Siegel got his share.

In addition to corn there were rows of tomatoes, green peppers, cabbage, carrots, and cucumbers, all in quantities too vast for their summer consumption. From mid-summer until fall was canning season. My grandmother had rows of shelves in their basement for storing canned fruits and vegetables.

My grandparents did not confine their farming to vegetables. They also had a gigantic strawberry patch. It is hard to place dimensions on such a patch decades after the fact, but I would guess it was around fifteen by forty feet in size. That required a lot of strawberry picking. Our parents loaned out my older brother and me for the occasion. I am sure our cousins, Jean and Bill Tanner, were also on the guest list.

Our reward was strawberry shortcake. This was similar to our corn on the cob meals. If there was anything on the menu besides strawberry shortcake, I no longer remember. We ate them with homemade biscuits. No one—and I mean no one—made biscuits better than my grandmother. These biscuits did not come from some tube in the refrigerator section of a supermarket. They were made by scratch and cut with a small-mouth mason jar. In my childhood innocence I feared only my grandmother knew how to make them—my mother surely didn't—and that when my grandmother died the knowledge of how to make biscuits would be lost forever.

The only other fruit they grew was raspberries. I was not fond of raspberries. They had thorns that reached out to grab you while you were trying to steal their fruit. Personally, I do not think the raspberries wanted to share. They were used mostly for jam. Grandma did not use fancy lids for her jam. Instead she used melted paraffin. That was the way her mother did it, and that was good enough for her. When I close my eyes I can still smell the mixture of sweet raspberry jam and hot paraffin. Our household got our share of the jam.

Sparta is in the center of a fruit belt, and my grandfather always knew a farmer who would let us pick cherries, pears, or peaches off the tree at reduced price. Guess who he invited to go along and help pick? Peaches were my favorite. Store-bought peaches can never compare with tree-ripened fruit. I always had my fill of fresh peaches before any went into the basket. Then my parents would be serving peaches and milk with every meal for weeks. If we were lucky—and we usually were—we would get invited to my grandparents' house for peach kuchen. I have since discovered that kuchen is German for cake. Much as I tried, I could never pronounce kuchen in the manner in which my grandfather expected it to be pronounced.

No farm is complete without livestock. If my grandparents had sufficient land, I am sure they would have acquired a dairy cow, so they could produce their own milk and make their own butter. They did have room for chickens. My grandfather purchased small chicks in the spring. I am guessing here, but there may have been as many as thirty chicks. To keep them warm, my grandfather made a hood from sheet metal. He placed a lightbulb in the center. He could regulate the heat by raising and lowering the hood. My grandparents looked at the chicks and saw future egg laying machines. My brothers and I looked at the chicks and saw immediate play toys. We were allowed to hold them under adult supervision, but they were not as much fun as a puppy or a kitten and the novelty quickly dissipated.

By mid-summer the chickens were moved from my grandparents' basement to an outside chicken coop. The chicken coop consisted of a small wooden shed with nesting boxes and an attached fenced-in run. I remember running down to the chicken coop when visiting my grandparents to search the nesting boxes for eggs. They were prolific hens, and I was seldom disappointed. I think my grandparents deferred collecting eggs when they knew I was coming to visit.

Occasionally, fried chicken was on the menu and not omelets. My grandfather would grab a chicken by the legs and drag it to a chopping block. A swift blow with his hatchet severed the head. As a young boy I should have found the procedure terrifying, but I was more intrigued by how a chicken could flop around the yard without its head.

One day five or six chickens were given death sentences. I no longer remember the occasion that called for so many chickens, but it was not because they were no longer laying eggs. We found several un-laid eggs still inside the chickens. The outer shells were soft or nonexistent. These eggs were saved along with the gizzard, heart, and liver. Nothing edible went to waste.

Once the decapitated chickens ceased flopping about, they were taken to the basement where a tub of boiling water waited. My grandfather dipped the chickens into the scalding water for a few seconds to loosen their feathers. My job was to pluck the feathers. Most of the feathers came off by the fistful without tearing the skin. The pinfeathers were a different story. Some of those had to be pulled with pliers. Scalded chicken feathers have a unique smell that I can remember to this day.

No account of my grandparents would be complete without describing my grandmother's cooking skills. She never made anything fancy or artistic, but boy did she excel at home cooking! She made everything from scratch. Egg noodles were rolled flat with a rolling pin and then cut into thin strips. Her homemade bread was kneaded by hand without the aid of a bread machine. Nothing smells better than grandma's homemade bread fresh from the oven. If Grandma had a cookbook, I never saw it. It was always a pinch of this and a dab of that—and her food always came out perfect.

There were two items for which she was famous (at least among grandkids). One was her pecan rolls. Every Easter (and sometimes on other holidays) our family was the recipient of a twelve-inch wheel of pecan rolls. These were made from flattened dough that was covered with sugar and cinnamon, and then rolled into a cylinder. The cylinder was cut into two-inch sections that were bunched together to form the twelve-inch wheel. The top was covered with a maple glaze and pecans before baking. My mouth is beginning to water just from writing about her pecan rolls.

Her other item of fame was her sugar cookies. They were huge! Maybe that is just the memory of an eight year old boy with small hands. In the center of each cookie was an oversized raisin. They almost looked like small prunes. I don't know where she got such large raisins. I have never seen them in stores. This may again be the faulty memory of a small child. What is not faulty is the fact that she possessed a magic self-filling cookie jar. It was never empty no matter how many grandchildren showed up at her door. I am sure all her grandchildren can attest to this fact.

My grandfather retired at age 65, although he worked as a part-time pastor for several years at the Kent City and Casnovia Methodist Churches. After many years of gardening, age began to take its toll. My parents said he would no longer have a garden during the coming summer. I was not surprised. Gardening required lots of work and was not as much fun after my grandmother died.

I confronted him about the garden one spring morning, well aware of what his answer would be—I came prepared. He told me severe arthritis in his knees prevented him from planting seeds and weeding the garden. Today, he would have had his knees replaced. He did not mention the recent death of his wife, but we both knew that was a factor.

I asked him if he would be willing to rent the land, as long as he was not planning to use it. I would repay him with all the vegetables he could consume. I expected to sell my share to my parents for a tidy profit and then help them eat the vegetables. We both got excited as we discussed the venture. We completed our agreement not with a handshake, but with two smiles. That was all that was needed between a grandfather and grandson.

That summer he would drag a lawn chair down to the edge of the garden where he directed my agricultural activities. I learned that corn requires lots of fertilizer, but if the fertilizer gets too close to the corn it will burn the roots. I formed a "V" shaped trench with the corner of my hoe between the rows of corn and filled it with fertilizer. He told me which crops are cold tolerant and could be planted early in the spring and which crops had to wait until after the last frost. I have planted many gardens since that summer, but none have been as productive as that garden with my grandfather.

The best part of that summer was the quality time I spent with my grandfather. He told me about growing crops on his boyhood farm using only oxen or plow horses. He told of listening to Civil War veterans tell about their battles. He told me of a woman from one of his churches who showed up at his door unannounced. She was crying and very distraught. She stayed over an hour, but when she left she was smiling and thanked my grandfather profusely for all his help. I asked him what he said to her that made such a difference. He said all he did was listen. He never said a word. I only wished I had asked more questions and taken notes.

Arthur Buege died in 1967 at age 82. I was in the military and unable to attend the funeral. I miss him.

2

Nash Creek

Small boys have a natural affinity for water, and I was no exception. Nash Creek flowed mere yards north of my grandparents' lot. It would become my playground whenever I visited them, which was often. My grandmother called it a river, although it was never more than eight or ten feet wide and seldom deeper than a foot except during spring floods—not a source of danger. My parents assumed I would stand up and save myself if I began to drown; it was that shallow. The creek continued through the town just north of Sparta's business section and finally dumped into Rogue River. Every spring we had flooding as the snow melted. Flood water covered my grandparents' garden with four or five feet of water. Their house was safe on a hilltop, but Harper Drive was submerged, stranding them for several days. Garter snakes and field mice took refuge at the edge of the flood water. Rogers Park and Balyeat Field were also inundated. Apparently, a narrow bridge over Nash Creek was the bottleneck that caused the flooding. The bridge was replaced and the flooding ceased.

My first memory of Nash Creek was when I was five or six and too young to play independently even by "free range" standards. Spring flooding had carved a vertical wall of sand on the far bank near a bend in the stream. The wall of hard-packed sand was no more than three feet tall, but that was sufficient for a colony of bank swallows to declare it home. I was fascinated by their graceful flight. I could watch them for hours, although with my childish attention span, it was more likely minutes. The swallows would twist and turn as they chased some unseen insect. Sometimes they would skim inches above the water to acquire a drink on the fly. Then to my amazement, they would fly up to the riverbank and then disappear into a hole in the sand.

It is unclear what caused their demise. Perhaps the nests were destroyed by two inquisitive brothers reaching into the holes to check out the nests. Or it could have been the natural erosion of the bank into a gradual slope that was unfit for bank swallows. Either way, they quickly disappeared from Nash Creek and were replaced by purple martins that lived in community housing created by my grandfather. His martin houses were legend within our family.

As we grew, my older brother and I were allowed to play along the creek unsupervised. Dairy cows trimmed the grass in the pasture and prevented weeds from growing along the creek banks, which let us crawl up to the water's edge and catch frogs, small turtles, and occasionally crabs. We called them crabs, but in reality they were crawfish.

Any portion of the creek that was too deep for us to see the bottom was immediately declared a "hole." We gave names to each hole, usually based on the type of fish inhabiting the hole. One such hole was no more than twenty feet from the corner of our grandparents' garden. We had to climb over a cattle fence, which was not a problem for young boys.

We called this the "Shiner Hole" because it was inhabited by a small fish that was noted for its shiny sides. The Shiner Hole was no more than thirty inches at its deepest spot. We were unable to see the bottom, but when a shiner turned sideways we could see a flash of light. My older brother and I had our first introduction to fishing at this hole. I don't specifically remember the equipment we used, but it was probably little more than fishing line attached to a small stick. Our goal was to catch shiners and sell them to Elmer Ryder's bait shop, which was a hundred yards farther downstream on North State Street. We earned little more than a penny or two for each minnow, and that was only if they were in perfect shape. We didn't realize it at the time, but Mr. Ryder was just being nice. I am sure he had commercial sources for bait minnows and did not need our business. He was picky in the minnows he did purchase. He required that we file the barb from our hooks to minimize damage to the fish. It was difficult finding hooks small enough for our purposes, and without barbs, we caught few minnows. We also sold night crawlers to Mr. Ryder—a penny for every two night crawlers. They likewise had to be in perfect shape. Elmer Ryder was willing to do business with children, but he never let us forget that it was a business.

As we grew older we moved up to larger fish. Farther upstream was a deeper hole that we called the "Sucker Hole." We had to climb over the cattle fence again and leave the pasture. A narrow trail through the brush followed the creek until it opened up at a bend of the river. The water at the Sucker Hole was close to four feet deep and was home to a school of suckers.

Suckers like carp are vegetarian bottom feeders. As such most people frown upon them as an edible fish. They are not as desirable as trout or walleye, but there is nothing wrong with them. They can be quite tasty when smoked. My grandmother had a theory that suckers are better in the spring when the water is cold. I doubt if this has any scientific merit, but she would still cook whatever we caught, and that included frog legs and crawfish tails. The frog legs were little more than flavored bone and the crawfish tails required cooking in a thick batter to make a bite out of them.

We took fishing for suckers more seriously. Our hooks were the proper size, and we left the barbs intact. For bait we used worms harvested from our grandfather's compost pile. There was always a pitchfork imbedded in the pile. One or two forkfuls produced all the worms we needed. Sometimes we used bobbers, but most of the time we just tossed our lines out and played along the river bank. Every few minutes we would pause to check our lines. Even though suckers are bottom feeding vegetarians, they do enjoy an occasional worm. We often caught three or four suckers in an afternoon. Most of the suckers were ten to twelve inches in length, but occasionally we caught suckers as long as sixteen inches.

Our productivity increased exponentially when my brother and I purchased a net from the profits of our ice cream route business (which will be explained in a future chapter). The net was about three feet tall and about six or seven feet wide. The ends were attached to poles, and we rolled up the net like a scroll when not in use. The bottom edge had lead sinkers to keep it down and the top had small corks to keep that end up. With my brother at one pole and me on the other pole, we dragged the net through the water. Since the river bottom was covered with stones and the occasional broken bottle, we always wore old tennis shoes.

We never knew what would turn up in the net. Sometimes we even caught snapping turtles, another reason for wearing tennis shoes. With a couple of sashays through the Shiner Hole, we could catch every shiner in the hole with minimal or no injury to the fish. We also caught a small fish that we called darters. They never got very big and Mr. Ryder had no interest in them. Even with the net, I doubt if we ever made more than a dollar selling minnows to Mr. Ryder.

Using the net on the Sucker Hole was more problematic. I don't know if the water was over my head, but parts of it came up to my chin. We did our best to straddle the deepest areas; even then it was difficult pulling the net through the water when the water was so deep. Sometimes we only spooked the suckers. The panicky fish swam wildly around in the muddy water and occasionally ran into our legs. It was enough to cause pain. The fish probably did not enjoy the encounter either. We had to walk downstream where the water was shallow to lift our net. It was not unusual to fill a pail with suckers after twenty minutes of netting.

One spring we hit the jackpot. My brother Jack and I and one of our neighbors—I can't remember if it was Jim Montgomery or his brother Wayne—were netting suckers in the Sucker Hole. We lifted the net and discovered a very large fish. It was a small mouth bass measuring fifteen or sixteen inches in length. Bass were unheard of in Nash Creek. They must have swum up from Rogue River.

Netting bass was illegal, but we were not about to return such a fine fish to the water. We never claimed to be angels. We placed the fish on a stringer and hid it in the water. Out of sight, out of mind. Unfortunately, one of the boys who lived in the neighborhood ran back to tell his father about the big fish we caught. Father and son soon returned to admire our fish. We held up one of the larger suckers. Surely, this was the fish the son was referring to. We continued netting in hopes that the father and son would lose interest and leave—they did not. As we lifted our net, to our horror and pleasure, we discovered two more similar sized bass. We did our best to play dumb, which was not hard. We proclaimed they were the strangest suckers we had ever seen. I don't think we fooled our spectator. He told us they were small mouth bass and large ones at that. He sensed our dilemma and told us it was OK to keep them, since we were only kids. After they left we snuck our fish home. They were delicious.

Suckers are migratory. Every March or April they swim up Nash Creek from the Rogue River or possibly even the Grand River to spawn. They do this at night to avoid predators. Little did they know my brother Jack and I were now nocturnal predators, and we were armed with spears. We did have our challenges. March and April were cold, and there was often ice and snow along the river banks. The water was too cold for swimming trunks and old tennis shoes. Waders or hip boots were a must. Fortunately, we were older and could afford better equipment. Jack had a driver's license, which made him armed and dangerous, but he did provide transportation for our expeditions. For reasons I no longer remember, we preferred spearing suckers on a section of Nash Creek west of Sparta near Peach Ridge. Perhaps it was merely to assert our independence.

During daylight, spawning suckers hid in deep pools where they cannot be seen, but during the night they swim farther upstream and into shallow water where we waited in ambush. We waded through foot-deep water carrying a Coleman lantern, which was bright enough to illuminate six feet in front of us. Any sucker within that range was clearly visible, although if they hugged the bank they were still difficult to see. Our spears had five barbed tines and were about four inches wide. When we saw a sucker we would slowly lower the spear until it was just above the sucker and then we pressed down against the river bottom. There was always lots of splashing of ice-cold water, but that was what made it fun. Some nights we wouldn't see any fish, other nights we might spear five or six.

Many people do not like to eat suckers. Some of this is cultural, but much of it is because of the small "Y" shaped bones that are finer than sewing thread. These bones frequently catch in the consumer's throat. There is a way to circumvent this problem that I learned from my grandfather. He would lay a fillet skin side down and then make lengthwise cuts a quarter inch apart. When fried, the hot grease would dissolve the small bones. We had neighbors who swore that the best way to eat suckers was smoked. Each to his own taste.

When I was in high school I tried my hand at trapping. The fur trade did not have the negative status it has today, and the price for fur was significant. I mostly trapped muskrats, but I always had visions of hitting the jackpot with a mink. It was a lot of work. I had to get up before school and check my trap line. This was done mostly in the dark. I did not make much money, but I got to play along my beloved Nash Creek.

There is an old saying that you can never return home. There is much truth to that statement. I have returned to my Nash Creek playground as an older adult and found it unrecognizable. Ryder's bait shop is gone. I am sure Mr. Ryder has retired to that big trout stream in the sky. The dairy farm is also gone. Without cows to trim the vegetation, brush and trees have overgrown the river bank making the water's edge unapproachable. Caretakers at Roger's Park no longer mow the grass and weeds along the bank. Brush has also overtaken this area, and it is no longer available to inquisitive children. In areas where I could view the river such as the bridge over North State Street, the water flow appeared to be half the volume it was during my childhood. I am sure the trees and brush around the water's edge divert a fair share of the water. My Nash Creek playground may be gone, but the memories will last forever.

3

B & T Dairy Bar

My father (Floyd Buege) was born in 1917 in Ferry, Michigan, where my grandfather was pastor of a small Methodist Church. Like his father, my dad enjoyed hunting and fishing and anything having to do with the outdoors. After graduating from high school he went to Ferris State College majoring in forestry. My brother remembers this differently, so this may be in error, but I remember seeing tree textbooks in our attic as a child. For reasons he never explained, he transferred to Michigan State College to pursue a degree in business.

My uncle (Lester Tanner) was working at a creamery in Caledonia during this time frame. He was looking for ways to advance his career, and there is no better way to advance a career than becoming the boss. He heard of a creamery in Sparta, Michigan that was for sale. Unfortunately, my uncle had a twelve-month commitment to his current job. Lester convinced my father to drop out of college after his third year and become Lester's partner in the dairy business. Money was tight and helping run a business offered an opportunity to use his business education.

The Tanner and Buege Dairy created a long business title. The new partners needed a shorter name to write on checks and other documents. They agreed to use their initials. Since Lester Tanner was the senior partner, the T & B Dairy was the logical choice, but tuberculosis was rampant in the 30s and 40s. They feared people would further shorten the name to TB Dairy.

It therefore became the B & T Dairy. It is possible the decision was based on alphabetical order, but the tuberculosis story is more plausible. Raw, unpasteurized milk was a major cause of TB.

There were no supermarkets in the late 1930s. Instead each neighborhood had a small grocery store with limited space to sell their wares. Most dairies and many bakeries sold directly to

B & T Dairy — Sparta Historical Commission Photo

the public. Prior to the 1930s milkmen transported raw milk in large containers and ladled out the desired amount to each consumer. To reduce outbreaks of tuberculosis and other milk-borne diseases, dairies switched to pasteurized milk in glass bottles.

During the first year, my father delivered milk during the week with my uncle driving up from Caledonia to help on weekends. They hand delivered milk for at least three years before switching to ice cream. We had a wooden milk box with a sloped hinged top on our front steps with room for four glass quarts. The thick, reusable glass bottles seldom broke. Each evening, my mother left our milk order partially protruding from the lid. My father, uncle, or later the Sealtest milk man placed the requested milk in the box. I assume she would leave money at the end of the week. A small circular piece of cardboard sealed the top of each bottle. A small tab created easy removal. No one envisioned anyone tampering with the milk.

The patent for homogenized milk dates back to 1899, but it was still rare in the 1950s. Cream naturally separates from milk and floats to the top, causing a demarcation line between the brighter white cream and the duller milk. If my mother needed cream for a recipe or for coffee she poured the cream off the top. If cream was not needed, she inverted the bottle several times to mix the milk and cream into whole milk. Cream was not a dirty word in the 1950s. Once the container was empty, it was thoroughly washed and returned to the milk box. No self-respecting housewife would return a dirty bottle to the milk box.

On Saturday, July 11, 1942 the B & T Dairy Bar officially opened its doors. Ice cream was a novelty and had to be eaten on the spot. Few people had refrigerators and sufficed with ice boxes refilled each day by the neighborhood ice man. Ice boxes kept meat and milk cold, but it did not prevent ice cream from melting. The Dairy continued to process and deliver milk for several more years. My uncle managed the milk business while my father ran the Dairy Bar. Eventually, it was decided that they could no longer compete with large dairies such as Sealtest. My uncle sold his portion of the business to my father and moved on.

The Dairy Bar produced a variety of hand-scooped ice cream flavors including butter pecan, chocolate, raspberry ripple, butter scotch marble, and many more. On the menu were such decadent items as banana splits, sundaes, and malted milk shakes made with a tablespoon of real malt. Malted milk shakes are impossible to find these days. Lastly, there were sodas. These were not the soft drinks southerners mistakenly call sodas. The "soda jerk" created a soda by placing chocolate or other flavor at the bottom of the container. Then a tablespoon or two of ice cream was mixed in. A high pressure stream of carbonated water sprayed into the mixture created a delicious liquid with a foam top. A scoop of ice cream completed the ensemble. If the customer brought his girlfriend, two straws were in order.

The lunch menu was limited to hamburgers and cheeseburgers, but who doesn't like a good cheeseburger. My father fried the hamburgers on a grill in a small alcove attached to the dining area. Sorry, no fries with that. Fast food and the customary fries had yet to make an appearance. There were no tables or booths, only swivel stools along a winding lunch counter. Glass containers scattered across the lunch counter provided paper straws to those in need. A metal rod connected the lid to the tray at the bottom of the glass container. When a customer lifted the lid, straws spread outward from the container. No plastic or paper covered the straws. They were clean and in the 50s that was sufficient preventive medicine.

Root beer was the drink of the era. The dairy did sell O-So grape and orange bottled "pop," but root beer on tap was the major draw. It was served in heavy glass mugs that were stored in the freezer. On a humid summer day, ice would form along the rim of the mug. I always enjoyed watching this ring of ice slide into the root beer. Root beer tasted best with a scoop of ice cream.

No date with a girlfriend was complete without a stop at the B & T Dairy for a sundae or banana split. The jukebox next to the pin ball machine worked overtime on Friday and Saturday evenings playing the latest hits. My father owned the pin ball machine, so my older brother and I could play for free after hours. It was our equivalent to today's video games.

Although the B & T was the hot spot in Sparta, the local A & W Root Beer drive-in provided competition in the summer. McDonalds and other fast food chains had yet to make a significant appearance. Root Beer stands were seasonal and true drive-ins. They offered no indoor seating. Customers drove up to the stand and rolled down the driver side window. A car hop (usually girls) would come up to the car and take the order. She would return with the ordered merchandise on a tray that could be attached to the partially-raised car window. Once the weather got cold, the drive-ins closed until the following summer. Many drug stores had year-round lunch counters. I remember often eating at a drug store in Grand Rapids in the 60s when I was matriculating at Grand Rapids Junior College.

During the winter of 1953-54 my father made a purchase. It arrived at the Dairy in a very large box. It was obvious some assembly was required. My older brother and I watched in fascination as our father put it together. We were unaware that we were to become part of the project. The largest segment consisted of a white insulated box with a small insulated door on the top. A pair of bicycle wheels on the sides and a smaller wheel in the front made the ice box mobile. My brother and I found quality entertainment pushing the contraption around the back of the Dairy. It was even more fun once our father added a handle bar in the rear with a row of noisy bells.

It wasn't until school let out for the summer that we discovered the true purpose of our ice box on wheels. My father placed metal discs of frozen brine in the bottom of the box and then loaded it up with popsicles, fudgesicles, and individual cups of ice cream with flavoring. According to the game plan, my brother and I were to push the wagon around Sparta and sell our cold merchandise to neighborhood children and adults. I was eight years old and my brother was eleven. It quickly became obvious that I was not an asset to the partnership. I am not sure if I even lasted a day.

My father found a ready replacement in our cousin, Bill Tanner, who was also the son of his former partner. Bill may have been in high school at the time and had plenty of muscle to push the cart. I am not sure if this is true, but I was told my brother often rode on top of the wagon while Bill pushed. My father opened a savings account for my brother, and by the end of the summer he had almost one hundred dollars in his bank account. That was a lot of money back in the mid-fifties. I was jealous.

The following year I was nine years old with dollar signs floating in my head. I wanted a piece of that fortune. I guess I was a capitalist at heart. I had to help push the cart while looking around the side like a train engineer, because I was still too short to look over the top. My brother watched from one side and I watched from the other. It took both of us to push the ice cream wagon up the hills.

Our pushcart was similar to the photo above except we had large fenders, which we stood on to reach inside the ice box. There was also a row of bells below the handle.

We had a well-defined route. We headed east on Division. This was mostly retail businesses where we made few sales. Then we turned south on Elm St. This residential street was home to many young children. We did not have to ring our bells very loudly to drum up business. At Gardner Street we headed east toward the Carnation factory where they canned condensed milk. We parked outside their side door similar to a modern day food truck and sold our cold desserts to the workers as they took their breaks. I was always fascinated by the cans rolling down the assembly line where labels were attached faster than the eye could perceive. Sometimes when business was slow, we played on the empty box cars or placed pennies on the tracks to get smashed—hey, we were just kids. If someone wanted to make a purchase, they would ring our bells, so we could run back and collect their money.

Sometime in the afternoon, I no longer remember the exact time, we headed over to the Extensole Factory on Aspen St. They manufactured wooden chairs and tables. Unlike the Carnation factory, they had a set break time. We parked beside their door and waited for the deluge. Sometimes we had so many customers that we just stood back while everyone helped themselves. They all knew the prices of our merchandise. We held open our black money bag for them to drop in the correct amount or make change. We knew we could trust the adults not to cheat us. We were not so sure about kids our age.

After the Extensole plant we headed to the Muskegon Piston Ring Foundry where we parked next to the guard house and sold our popsicles and other cold delights to the factory workers coming and going. Then it was west to State St., past our house, and back to the Dairy.

When noticing our age, many people would wonder about sweat shops and child labor laws. I later learned that child labor laws did not apply to family members. I am not sure if this included our cousin Bill, but he did not complain nor did anyone else. Like any worker we grumbled about going to work until payday arrived. We individually earned between seven and ten dollars a week. Farm kids our age did chores for a lot less money. We also had control of an entire icebox filled with cold treats, which made us the envy of our peers.

We were undoubtedly the richest kids in the neighborhood. Case in point: Our neighbor owned a vacant lot behind our house where we played softball. She wanted to sell the lot, which would terminate the use of our playing field. My parents were willing to pay $200 for the lot, but the neighbor wanted $250. After a handshake my older brother and I agreed to pay the extra $50 on land contract. How many kids our age were land barons? Every week we would march next door to make our payment. It took much of our summer earnings, but it was worth it. At the end of the summer we were part owners of a ballfield.

4

Halloween

Halloween was one of my favorite holidays. I didn't believe in ghosts, goblins or other spiritual entities. I didn't believe in All Hallows' Eve as a Christian recognition of those who had passed away. I didn't believe Halloween was a sacrilegious pagan celebration to be avoided. I did believe in having a good time, and that alone was sufficient reason for celebrating Halloween.

No Halloween observance was complete without jack-o'-lanterns on the front steps. Since my parents had four kids, it was imperative that we had four jack-o'-lanterns. We carved the pumpkins several days before Halloween to provide sufficient time for neighbors to fully appreciate our budding artistic talent. Our parents even let us use paring knives. I can't remember anyone cutting a finger, but my memory has diminished with age. Being boys we did our best to create gruesome faces, which meant the jack-o'-lanterns had large, square teeth and a downturned mouth. Pumpkins did not qualify as jack-o'-lanterns until we placed a burning candle inside the pumpkin. Then we left them on the front steps. I think I would have remembered if anyone had smashed or otherwise vandalized our pumpkins. Pumpkin smashing was not a popular sport during the '50s.

In the lower elementary grades we were allowed to wear costumes to school. Girls preferred ballerinas and fairies. Tinkerbell was a favorite among the girls. Boys preferred grotesque and scary. I remember one classmate showing up in long underwear. It was unclear what kind of statement he was trying to make, but we all thought he should be embarrassed. We were just learning modesty and underwear was not to be exposed. When a girl performed a summersault on the monkey bars and exposed her panties, the boys noted the color. We knew that was important and sensitive information although none of us knew why.

At the beginning of class the teacher paraded us to the front where we showed off our costumes. We took pride in having the best costume. Our family had a box filled with an assortment of rubber masks and fake wigs that we recycled each year. By mixing and matching we could create a different costume each year. The rubber masks were hot, and it was difficult peering through the small eye openings. Once everyone in the classroom had seen our costumes, most of us removed the essentials; we still had a day of classwork.

If we were lucky our teacher might organize a Halloween party for the end of class. She would coordinate the party with several parents who agreed to bring Halloween-themed cookies and cupcakes. The treats were invariably prepared in home kitchens unapproved by the local health department. No one got sick, and I am sure the home-cooked treats were superior to commercial cookies and cakes.

Halloween did not become serious until late in the day. Where I live today, trick or treating has to be completed before dark. In Sparta during the '50s, trick or treating did not begin until dark. Darkness added to the atmosphere of the holiday. We were ghosts and goblins. We were supposed to be scary. Darkness augmented that illusion. Before Daylight Saving's Time, the sun set at a quarter to six on Halloween.

Sparta is a farming community and many kids lived on farms. Trick or treating is not as rewarding when the houses are spaced a half mile apart. Those of us living in town discovered we had lots of friends. Farm kids arrived by carloads accompanied by their parents. My father would make sloppy joes. They were easy to make, and he had access to an unlimited supply of buns from the B & T. Our guests often brought donuts and cider, which were a Halloween tradition.

Sometimes the adults would organize an apple dunking contest for us. We had an old wash tub that they filled with water for the occasion. Apples float in water. The object was to grab one of the floating apples using only our teeth. It looks easy, but when a contestant tried to grab an apple he merely pushed the apple under the water. The only way to win was to dive in head first and pin an apple against the bottom of the tub. Needless to say it was a great spectator sport that required a mop and bucket for clean-up.

Once it became sufficiently dark we donned our masks and grabbed a paper bag; it was time for trick or treating. Our parents expected that my older brother and I would take our younger brothers with us. We did this begrudgingly, but we knew it would soon be past their bed time. We would still have plenty of evening to enjoy. While we went trick or treating the adults played cards or just socialized. It was party time for them too.

The treats we received were a mixture of homemade and store bought. Homemade taffy was popular, as were Halloween themed cookies wrapped in cellophane. My grandmother was famous for her popcorn balls. Our loot was never inspected by our parents, although we did suspect they may have searched our treats for their favorite goodies after we went to bed. No one imagined that someone would place a razor blade or needle in a child's candy. That was unthinkable in the 1950s.

This may be hard to believe, but even a kid can get tired of collecting candy. Eventually our bags became heavy, and the novelty of trick or treating began to wear off. We returned to home base and discharged our younger brothers. But the night was yet young.

We dumped our candy and costumes and headed back into the night. There were invariably five or six of us—all boys. We headed toward Division Street, which was the business district in Sparta. It was a half-mile walk. I don't remember any girls, but all the boys gathered in downtown Sparta. The boys in our group represented multiple ages. Whomever we met was always a classmate of someone in our group. It was a small town.

Soaping windows was a primary source of entertainment. We each had a bar of soap, and the large windows on retail establishments was our canvas. We drew pictures, wrote jokes, and added what we thought were words of wisdom. This was not considered vandalism. Police cruisers patrolled the streets, but the city police preferred issuing candy, not citations. Store owners rationalized that their windows needed washing anyway. If we soaped windows on any other day, I am sure we would have been in trouble.

My memory may again be faulty, but I don't remember any four-letter words written on the windows. Such words were not socially acceptable in the '50s. People did not talk about "F" bombs on radio and TV. Newspapers did not print s*** as if the asterisks somehow sanitized the use of vulgar language. If we had come across such words, we would have erased them to rectify a wrong.

We had a moral code. Soaping residential windows was out of bounds. They belonged to the people who give us candy, but merchant widows were fair game. Soap was an acceptable writing tool; sealing wax was not. The theory was that merchants could easily wash off soap, but wax was difficult to remove. I was never sure of the veracity of that claim, but we were ready to vilify anyone caught using sealing wax.

Malicious destruction of property was also considered unacceptable behavior. One Halloween Wayne Montgomery, who was a neighbor, and I were walking past an abandoned creamery just north of the Nash Creek bridge on Union Street. Since it had been abandoned for several years, it obviously had to be haunted. With flashlights in hand we decided to explore. We found an unlocked door and entered the building. All the rooms were empty and filled with cobwebs, which was a major disappointment. It was also devoid of ghosts, but that would change when we told the story to our friends. We had just exited the building when a police officer pulled up in a patrol car. He asked if we had been inside the building. My response would have been, "What building?" Unfortunately, Wayne answered first and 'fessed up to our crime. The officer informed us that we were guilty of breaking and entering. We informed the officer that we were only guilty of entering, since we did not break anything. It was not nice to break other people's property. He countered that opening an unlocked door constituted breaking and entering. I countered that the door was partially open and technically we did not open it. To this day I do not remember if it was partially open or not. We didn't have Perry Mason to defend us, so we did the best we could. We must have looked innocent as he let us off with a stern warning. On Halloween police do not look for trouble. I am sure he was more concerned about us getting hurt inside the building. As long as everyone behaved in a civil manner, the police were willing to bend the rules for one night.

When not soaping windows or discussing legal theory with local cops, we devised harmless, but diabolical, pranks. The classic prank was to hide behind a tree trunk next to the sidewalk. Trees in Sparta are old with thick trunks, and we were small. Hiding behind the trees was easy. In the '50s we had few street lights. The sidewalks were dark. When a trick or treater came even with the tree we would jump out and yell. It was impossible not to be startled even though everyone was familiar with the ploy. It was good for a laugh, even better if the trick or treater was a classmate or friend. Afterword it was wise to take off running.

One Halloween we devised the perfect prank. I don't know who came up with the idea, but the instigators included my older brother Jack, my cousin Ward Morrill from Benton Harbor, a future deputy sheriff and neighbor Jim Montgomery, and me. The plan required birds. My partners in crime were quick to suggest we use one of my homing pigeons that I raised. I nixed this suggestion; homing pigeons would snitch on me by returning to my loft.

Jim Montgomery, the future deputy sheriff, happened to know of an auto garage with low hanging eaves. He was pretty sure there were sparrows roosting in the eaves. Armed with small brown paper bags we headed for the garage. It took us about twenty minutes, but we were able to "harvest" four or five sparrows. Our perfect prank was beginning to take shape.

Every Halloween the Sparta Theater scheduled the scariest movie they could find. It was considered too intense for younger children and older children would not dare be seen with their parents. Consequently, only older kids attended the movie. One of us purchased tickets for the entire group. We entered the lobby and bypassed the popcorn stand. We did not wish to press our luck. We pushed past the ticket taker with tickets in outstretched arms. We wanted to keep him occupied with collecting tickets. We made it into the darkened theater with our contraband undetected.

We were supposed to watch a scary movie, but no one was in a mood to be scared. Kids were climbing over chairs. Some were playing the classic game of "steal the hat." There were always a few kids who smuggled in water balloons—amateur pranks. The ushers didn't mind. They had our money and the theater was sold out. They could clean up the mess in the morning after they took our money to the bank.

About fifteen minutes into the movie, the sparrows escaped—on cue. There were no perches on which to land other than the disc-shaped deco lights on the walls. For the most part, the sparrows flew around the theater. When a bird flew in front of the projector, the shadow of a prehistoric monster flew across the screen. It was more impressive than the *Giant Claw*. Every time a bird flew across the screen, the audience applauded. We were ready to stand up and take a bow, but no one would have seen us in the dark. We had pulled off the perfect Halloween prank. Our accomplishment would be told around campfires for years to come.

5

Movie Theater

Sparta Movie Theater

Like many small towns, Sparta offered a one-screen movie theater. It sat on the north side of E. Division Street at the far end of the business district. I no longer remember the adult fare, but in the mid '50s a nickel and a dime provided admission for children under twelve. Without video games or TVs to entertain us, my older brother and I relished the half-mile walk to the theater and the return trip in the dark—all unattended. I was eight or nine and my brother Jack was three years older. This may seem like child neglect by today's standards, but we were free-range children as were most children in the '50s. We had no TV or Internet to flaunt worldly evils. If a child were brutally assaulted in California or New York, it never made headlines in our local paper. I never feared walking home in the dark, although I don't remember ever going to the theater without my brother. Our parents assumed there was safety in numbers.

We lined up to purchase our tickets at the ticket booth located outside the theater. Fortunately, we had overhead cover to protect us from the elements. While we were in line we were "forced" to look at the two large glass-enclosed posters that hawked coming feature movies. The movies changed twice a week, with one movie playing Sun-Mon-Tue and another movie from Wed thru Sat. A popular movie could last a week or longer, but this was unusual.

Once we had ticket in hand, we entered the theater through one of three large double doors that led to the concession area. Our nostrils were immediately overwhelmed by the smell of freshly-popped corn. I remember being mesmerized by the staccato sound as the popcorn overflowed the cooking kettle. No movie was complete without a bag of freshly popped corn. We didn't have buckets in those days. The popcorn was sold in highly decorated bags, and the price was reasonable.

Ushers collected our tickets as we entered the main theater by one of two doors. Each door led to an aisle that separated the seating into three sections. The floor of the theater sloped down toward the big screen, so everyone had an unobstructed view. Six colorful deco lights lined the walls. These were disc shaped and perhaps a foot in diameter. Red, yellow, and possibly other colors radiated out like spokes on a wagon wheel. They added atmosphere to the theater and provided sufficient light during the movie so patrons could navigate down the aisle. I am not sure but I believe after the end of the movie, bright white lights replaced the colored lights to fully illuminate the theater as people made their way to the exit.

When we went to the movie theater we expected an evening of entertainment, and we were never disappointed. They were mostly double features. The entertainment began with a "B-movie," which was a low budget film normally less than seventy minutes in length. They seldom made it to the glass-encased posters outside the theater. Occasionally, they would be promoted by title as an afterthought. B-movies were normally in black and white and did not have the highest paid actors, although some up and coming actors such as John Wayne and Jack Nicholson began their careers in B-movies.

The B-movies often followed a repeating theme with the same actors playing the same hero, albeit a different plot. Westerns were one of the staples. Romance was never part of a western in the fifties. At the end of the movie when the hero had to choose between the girl and his horse, he invariably chose his horse and rode off into the sunset. When I was eight, I totally agreed with his choice.

A newsreel documentary followed the B-movie. These were two or three minute black and white films showing the christening of a new warship or footage of steeplejacks building a new skyscraper. The clips were narrated without dialogue from the participants. The newsreel documentaries faded from the screen in the mid-fifties as television became a household fixture.

An animated cartoon was also expected between the B-movie and the featured film. Looney Tunes and Merrie Melodies provided the lion's share of the cartoons. Some of the rising stars included Daffy Duck, Porky Pig, Tom & Jerry, Bugs Bunny, Tweety Bird, Elmore Fudd, and Yosemite Sam. We all had our heroes. I rooted for Wile E. Coyote, but it was always in vain. Even with his superior imagination and effort, he always fell short. At the end of a Looney Tunes cartoon, Porky Pig would pop out of a drum and say, "Th-th-that's all, Folks."

The lights would come on: Intermission Time. We had been sitting for close to an hour and a half. It was time to use the bathroom. Boys and men would use the bathroom on the left and girls and women would line up on the right. There was no potty parity in the '50s. Management also hoped we would replenish our popcorn and soft drinks.

After about fifteen minutes the lights would dim for the main feature. The main features were as likely westerns as not, but they were in color and had big name actors such as Roy Rogers or Gene Autry. There was lots of violence with fist fights, shoot-em ups, and brawls, but I never saw any blood. When Roy Rogers drew his pistols and fired at the bad guys, their guns would fly out of their hands. The villains would grab their gun hand as if in pain, but Roy's bullet always missed their fingers and hit the gun. Fist fights invariably ended when one of the participants was knocked out. Sometimes an actor was knocked out when hit in the head with the butt of a pistol. Either way, it only took a pail of cold water poured over the head to bring them out of the deepest coma. I often wondered why that never worked in the ER. It would have been so much faster than going through the coma protocol.

With all that fighting do you think there was any profanity or four-letter words? Nope! If there were R-rated movies, they never came to Sparta. Most movies were family films that could be enjoyed by the entire family. I remember my parents taking my older brother and me to see the *Shaggy Dog*, the *Nutty Professor*, and *Old Yeller* (very sad ending). My two younger brothers were not old enough to enjoy a movie, so they were left with a baby sitter.

Even though there were no R-rated movies, there were some movies our parents preferred we not see. These mostly fell into the science fiction or horror categories. I am sure they feared we would have nightmares. If we wished to see a film that fell into one of those categories we had to resort to parent psychology. We had the upper hand, since we monitored the glass enclosed posters at the movie theater and knew the name of the film. Our parents normally didn't have a clue. As dutiful parents they would ask the name of the movie we wished to see. As children with early Alzheimer's, we confessed that we couldn't remember the title (little white lie), but it was a really good movie. We could easily remember the title of the B-Movie, which invariably was a benign western. As a clincher, we would add that there would be a cartoon (there was always a cartoon). Since we had our own money that we earned from our pushcart ice cream business we usually won out. We got to see the *Giant Claw* about a huge bird from outer space that was crushing airliners. The acting was excellent, but the ferocious bird looked like it escaped from Sesame Street. It had audiences laughing. The *Giant Claw* is now rated as one of the worst science fiction movies of the fifties. Needless to say neither my brother nor I had any nightmares.

We were not always confined to the movies available at the Sparta Theater. Sometimes our parents would load us up in the station wagon and head for one of several drive-in theaters. Even my younger brothers were allowed to go, although they frequently fell asleep in the car before the end of the movie. This was before daylight savings time, so it got dark much earlier in the summer. We would drive into the sequestered area behind the big screen and select a row. The rows were all inclined upward, so after we parked the car we had a good view of the screen. Speakers hung on posts between adjacent cars. We would hang the speaker on the driver's or passenger's window depending on which side of the post we parked. Each speaker had its own volume control. The acoustics were not great by today's standards, but we didn't care.

Some of the movie theaters had playgrounds at the base of the giant screen. If we arrived early, Jack and I were allowed to play on the swings and slides. We knew we were to return to the car as soon as the movie began. Sometimes it was difficult to find our car in the dark, but I never remember getting seriously lost.

A large concrete building sat in the center of the parking area. This building housed the projection room. I never saw the projector, but it must have been enormous to illuminate such a large screen from a long distance. The building also offered bathrooms. There was always a line up for the bathrooms if I remember right. The concession stand was usually in the back of the building. They sold candy, soft drinks, and popcorn.

We never purchased anything from the concession stand. One of the advantages of a drive-in theater was that we could bring our own refreshments. We arrived with a grocery bag filled with popcorn. My father made the best popcorn. He began with bacon grease in the bottom of a large cooking pan. Then he added the popcorn. Once the popcorn began to pop, he would shake the pot to ensure that gravity pulled the un-popped kernels toward the bacon grease at the bottom of the pan. Eventually the popcorn began to overflow like it did in the movie theater. My father would then lift the lid so the popped corn fell into a waiting bowl. A little salt and butter transformed it into the perfect movie snack. Today it would be impossible to eat such popcorn guilt-free, but bacon grease did make the best tasting popcorn.

The sixties opened new avenues of entertainment. I now had a driver's license and enjoyed my independence. I no longer needed my parents to chauffeur me to a drive-in theater or the Majestic Theater in Grand Rapids. Now I had a choice of movies. Sometimes I went with teen-age friends. Sometimes I went with a date. Either way, I felt worldly with my new-found mobility.

The Majestic Theater was the epitome of the large screen movie theater. It had a seating capacity of 1,200 with 700 on the main floor and the rest in the two balconies. I am not sure about the screen size, but it rose almost to the third floor level. Before the movie and during intermission a twin-chambered Barton Theater Organ would rise up from the orchestra pit and entertain the crowd. Pillars of red velvet hung from the sides of the auditorium. Matching red curtains covered the screen. When the red curtains parted you knew quality entertainment was moments away.

Televisions became an entertainment staple in the early to mid '50s. They combined the best of radio and cinema. Radio shows such as *The Lone Ranger* and *Roy Rogers* easily made the transition to TV and became my favorites. The silver screen's newsreels played well on TV without any change. They gradually transitioned to live news feed. Newsreels and B-movies faded from the theater scene.

Badgerows who lived two doors north of us were the first in the neighborhood to purchase a TV. I only got to see it once. The screen was circular like an oscilloscope and about eight inches in diameter. Programing was sporadic. I think we bought our first TV around 1952. The screen was much bigger and square with rounded corners. This was before transistors and integrated circuits. Operation of the TV was dependent on multiple vacuum tubes that frequently burned out. They required TV repairmen who could come to the house and replace the tubes. Fortunately, our neighbor was a TV repairman. I believe he learned much of his electronic skills during World War II.

We received two channels that were dependent on the whim of the rabbit ears on top of the TV. These were nothing more than two metal rods reaching upward in a "V" formation. Conventional wisdom was that draping tin foil between the ears would improve reception. I don't remember if it made much of a difference. Sometimes the picture would roll and we would see the bars separating the picture frames scrolling across the screen. Or the picture might slant sideways and obscure all remnants of the pictures. These responded to various tuning knobs on the TV. We later advanced to a chimney antenna. This antenna had a motor with controls on top of the TV that would rotate the antenna for best reception. My parents did not get a color TV until after I had left the nest.

TV proved to be just as addicting as today's electronics. We rushed home after school to watch such programs as the puppet show *Kukla, Fran, and Ollie*. This program became as popular with adults as with children. The Howdy Doody Show was another popular afterschool program, which featured Buffalo Bob as host and a marionette named Howdy Doody. There was also a mute clown named Clarabell played by Bob Keeshan who later became Captain Kangaroo. In 1955 Mickey Mouse Club hit the airwaves and was an immediate success. Unfortunately, it only aired for three years because the network wanted more advertising and Walt Disney refused.

On Saturday there was an entire morning of kids' shows. We watched Captain Midnight, sponsored by Ovaltine, Sky King, Gene Autry, The Cisco Kid, The Lone Ranger, Hop-Along Cassidy, and Roy Rogers. Very few shows, whether kid shows or adult shows, were an hour long. Most were a half hour.

Around ten or eleven o'clock at night the networks would play the National Anthem and cease broadcasting for the night. A test pattern filled the screen until morning.

6

Medical Care

According to MapQuest, Spectrum Hospital in Grand Rapids is sixteen miles from downtown Sparta. It only takes twenty-three minutes on four-lane highways to make the drive to a hospital capable of handling any emergency. This was not always the case. In the 1950s, M-37 was a two-lane road that meandered between Sparta and Grand Rapids. Once in Grand Rapids, a lengthy commute through urban streets awaited the driver heading toward the nearest hospital. The entire trip could consume an hour.

Consequently the Sparta community was for the most part medically independent. We had our own medical center managed by Drs. Thomas Fochtman and Frank Bull. They maintained office hours at their medical center on Division Street, but one of them was always on call after routine office hours. They also made house calls. I remember one evening when my grandfather collapsed just as we were about to sit down to dinner. I was a small child at that time and was told little other than it was probably a heart attack. At my age I could only watch. My grandfather was carried to a nearby bed. No one called 911. They called Dr. Fochtman or Dr. Bull. The doctor arrived with black bag in hand. My grandfather had returned to consciousness before his arrival. The physician took his pulse and probably his blood pressure. He listened to my grandfather's heart with his stethoscope. No EKG was ordered.

No trip to the ER in Grand Rapids. Whatever the physician did must have been adequate as my grandfather lived for many more years.

I can remember only two visits to the Doctor's office in my early youth. One was for a severe foot infection and the other time I stepped on a nail. Both were declared emergencies by the medical receptionist, as we were told to use the back door of the medical building. (The back door was reserved for emergencies.) I did have a bout of pneumonia diagnosed by stethoscope—no X-ray. This was diagnosed over two house calls.

In the 1940s it was common for communities such as Sparta to have uncertified birthing centers. When a woman went into labor, Drs. Fochtman or Bull sent her to the Anderson Maternity Home, which was a residential home in Sparta. The home owner reserved a small room for deliveries. No formally trained staff was needed as the doctor was expected to deliver the baby, but experience is often the best instructor. The owner of the home provided all pre and post-delivery care. I was born in the transition period when hospitals were replacing uncertified birthing centers. The Anderson Maternity Home closed soon after my older brother was born, but my mother asked the owner if she would remain open for my mother's next pregnancy. The woman promised she would. The birthing center closed, but true to her word, the owner reopened long enough for me to enter the world. I believe I was the last planned delivery in Sparta.

Most medical problems were treated by Dr. Mom. No one went to the doctor for upper respiratory infections and that included strep throat. Penicillin was discovered by Alexander Fleming in 1928, but physicians didn't begin using it to treat infections until 1942. It slowly became available to rural physicians in the early 1950s. When we got a sore throat we suffered at home. Treatment consisted of over-the-counter cough medications. I still remember severe ear pain treated only with aspirin. The treatment of choice for nausea was Coca Cola syrup from soda fountain of the local drug store. This was basically Coca Cola without the soda water. I remember this worked well for nausea. There is still medical and scientific rational for its effectiveness. Peppermint oil was used for stuffy noses. My mother would place a drop or two on the lapel of my pajamas. When my nose became plugged I would sniff the peppermint oil. I don't know if this was placebo effect or not, but it seemed to work.

Any injury short of an amputation was treated at home. Cuts and scratches were treated with the dreaded tincture of iodine and a Band-Aid. The iodine made any injury ten times more painful. This was probably caused by the alcoholic base. I remember blowing on the cut after the iodine was applied helped relieve the burning sensation. This probably caused the alcohol to evaporate more quickly. Then a miracle occurred; someone invented Mercurochrome. Mercurochrome painted the wound red just like iodine but it didn't sting or burn like iodine. It contained mercury; however, mercury was not poisonous in the fifties. We had thermometers filled with mercury, and we played with the liquid metal in chemistry class. When at school and Dr. Mom was unavailable, Dr. Teacher took over. There were no school nurses. With recess twice a day there was always someone with a scratch or cut. Dr. Teacher would pull out her medical bag filled with Q-tips, Band-Aids, and Mercurochrome and provide the same care as Dr. Mom would at home. There was no fear of lawsuits. We all survived. In 1998, Mercurochrome was deemed ineffective and removed from the market.

Schools partnered with the county health department to provide diphtheria, tetanus and pertussis vaccinations. It was rare for a child to get these vaccinations from their local physician. Parental permission was still required, but few parents opted out. Parents assumed scientists and physicians knew more about medicine than they did. I think I was the only Anti-Vaxxer in the fifties—I hated needles. Teachers gave permission slips to the students to take home for the parents to fill out. Mine always got lost on the way home. Unfortunately, my older brother dutifully brought his home, which led to my cross examination.

The last case of smallpox in the United States was reported in 1949, but because of the world-wide threat we still received vaccinations. The smallpox vaccination was unlike other vaccinations. Instead of a needle the nurse placed a droplet of vaccine on the shoulder and then punctured the outer skin layer with a two-pronged needle, forcing the vaccine just under the skin. After a few days a vesicle developed over the site if the vaccine "took." If not the procedure was repeated. Some individuals with very active immune systems developed dime-sized blisters that left permanent scars. After 1971 the CDC no longer recommended smallpox vaccination in the U.S. Naturally occurring smallpox was declared extinct on May 8, 1981.

One of the greatest health concerns in the fifties was polio. The illness occurred more frequently in the spring and filled the hearts of parents with fear. I was too young to share this fear, but I do remember pictures of children in iron lungs. Iron lungs looked like large metal canisters that engulfed the entire patient except for the head. It was not much of a lifestyle for a child, but it helped the patients breathe and stay alive.

In 1955 Jonas Salk perfected a new vaccine for polio and needed lab animals to test the medicine. The school in Sparta was one of the chosen sites, and we were the lab animals. Naturally, they needed parental permission. My permission slip got lost on my way home, but the new vaccine was the talk of the town and my parents found out. "He would be happy to volunteer," they said. They had four sons and could spare one for such a worthy cause. This required not one shot but also required a booster shot. The vaccine was a remarkable success. Such a test is of little value unless there is a control to compare it with. A few months later, my parents were informed I was part of the control and received a saline shot and not the polio vaccine. The health nurse returned with needle in hand to vaccinate all students in the control group. After the project was over, participants were given cards proclaiming us "Polio Pioneers." I treasured that card for many years.

Eventually even small towns have emergencies requiring an ambulance with lights and siren. Sparta was no exception. Our ambulance service was run by the Hessel Funeral Home, which was next door to the medical center. This may sound like conflict of interest for a funeral home to operate an ambulance, but this was common in the fifties. Morticians were always on call and had training in anatomy and physiology. In 1966 I worked for a professional ambulance company in Grand Rapids. I only needed standard and advanced first aid, which I was taught on a Saturday afternoon. I could not drive the ambulance because drivers had to be twenty-one with a chauffeur's license. I am sure the morticians were better trained than I was.

John Badgerow and I walked home from school every day. Not that we were in a hurry to get home, but we took a shortcut that meandered behind the Ben Franklin Store, the Medical Center, and the Methodist and Baptist Churches. Being inquisitive kids, we often checked the garbage can behind the Medical Center. Mostly we found old bloody bandages and paper products, but occasionally we would find used syrettes. In the 1950s most needles and syringes were autoclaved and reused. What we found were single-use syrettes. Rubber plungers were lodged at the bottom of the syrettes. A small threaded rod protruded from each plunger. We assumed a reusable missing piece screwed onto this rod to make the plunger movable.

Without that missing piece, the syrettes were useless, but we "borrowed" a handful of syringes anyway. When we got home we broke one of the syrettes to further examine the rubber plunger. I don't remember if it was my idea or John's, but we discovered that the end of a ball-point pen refill fit nicely over the small threaded rod. Then when we crimped it with a pair of pliers, the ink cylinder took the shape of the threaded rod. We could now thread it over the unbroken threaded rods; we had a new play toy! We squirted each other and injected water into a variety of substances.

Any nurse, physician, or physician assistant including me will be horrified upon reading about our activities. We were kids being kids. I also do not fault Drs. Fochtman or Bull. We were growing up before HIV/AIDS, and they were following the medical standard for the 1950s, where all bloody bandages and used syringes went to the local landfill. Bottom line: we survived.

7

Sparta

The arrival of the railroad in the late 1800s turned a small, rural settlement of farmers into a village with industrial potential. Companies could now ship their goods anywhere in the nation. By the 1950s rail cars were hauling freight for the Muskegon Piston Ring, the Carnation Canning Company, and the Extensole furniture factory. As I remember they were the three major factories within the village limits. What could not be seen was the vast agricultural business surrounding Sparta. Agriculture probably did more to support Sparta's retailers than the three major industries combined.

Retail stores were mostly confined to Division St, although there were a few businesses located on State St. and Union St. near their intersections with Division. Almost anything could be purchased in Sparta. The village offered several car dealerships, two hardware stores, a butcher shop, two drug stores, and two banks. The Ben Franklin store occupied the southwest corner of Division and Union streets. Sometimes we called it a Dime Store or the Five and Ten (cents). They sold everything. I fondly remember the bulk candy bins that greeted customers as they entered the store. Goldfish were available in the back of the store along with other pet supplies. Occasionally, even small turtles were available for purchase. In between were yard goods, curtain rods, softballs, cap pistols, and pea shooters. Marbles of every kind graced the shelves every spring.

Ben Franklin, AKA Dime Store — Sparta Historical Commission Photo

We didn't have Amazon, but we did have a Sears and Roebuck catalogue. It had over a thousand pages of merchandise from clothing to farm equipment. If what you wanted could not be found in the local retail stores, it was invariably available in the Sears and Roebuck catalogue. My father, who had large feet, purchased his shoes from the catalog. I fondly remember flipping through the toy section every fall as Christmas approached. When not used for ordering merchandise, it made an excellent booster seat for small children who found it difficult eating at the dinner table. Since the catalogue came out twice a year, it was disposable and often found its way to outhouses.

Credit cards were nonexistent in the '50s. Customers paid for their merchandise with cash or check. In place of bonus points or rewards, shopkeepers dispensed green stamps. Most men found little interested in the postage-sized, green stamps, but they knew better than to throw them away. They dutifully gave them to their spouses who pasted them into books. With a large purchase, a customer could get a sheet of stamps. A small catalogue displayed a variety of merchandise redeemable with the books of stamps. Two books might get you a toaster, and five books might get you a vacuum sweeper. The closest redemption center was in Grand Rapids. I think it was either Wurzburgs or Herpolsheimers.

Without the Internet, there was no e-mail. All paper correspondence required the services of the U.S. Post Office. The Post Office was somehow able to deliver an out of state envelope to the correct household in Sparta without the aid of zip codes—and they did this for a three-cent stamp. Kathy Lang, who was a classmate of mine, tells a humorous story from decades ago. Someone sent a card to her parents addressed to: Tony and Doris, Sparta Michigan and it was delivered to them. That was how small Sparta was.

Tipping in the '50s was the exception and not the rule. If lunch came to $2.75, that was what the waitress expected. If the customer was feeling generous or the waitress provided exceptional service, the customer might tell the waitress to keep the change, or a few coins might be left next to the plate. Over the years, the tip has become the expectation, with the value determined as a percentage of the bill. What began as ten percent has inflated to fifteen, and now twenty percent. Often for large groups the tip is included in the bill for the "convenience of the customer."

Other than the local movie theater there was little to entertain Sparta residents during the 1950s. Televisions were expensive and had only meager programming. Radios provided quality news, but the sound was of low quality. Local residents found it necessary to entertain themselves.

Retail stores closed around six o'clock on most evenings, but Friday evenings were party time, and the stores remained open until nine o'clock. Everyone with nothing to do on a Friday night gathered downtown for window shopping and general socialization. It was common to find the park benches along Division St. filled with people chatting up neighbors or waving at friends as they drove by.

A public drinking fountain on the northeast corner of Division and Union streets catered to thirsty individuals. The fountain was constructed of concrete embedded with small stones. Water bubbled up continuously from a central pipe. There was no face guard on the pipe. In those days we did not worry about someone placing their mouth around the faucet—and no one got sick.

A village park with large trees and a band shell occupied the west side of the corner. I don't remember any concerts in the park, but I am sure the high school band played there in the spring. My only memory of the park was watching bulldozers push over the large, majestic trees to make way for a bank. It filled me with sadness to see the trees fall even at such a young age.

The fire station was across the street from the B & T Dairy and just north of the park. It was operated by volunteer firemen. There were no cell phones or pagers to call the firemen. Instead, a large siren protruded from the top of the fire station. When the siren sounded, people could hear it from most locations within the village. I often had a front-row seat at the B & T Dairy when the alarm sounded. It was amazing to watch grown men run toward the fire hall. This was before the jogging for health phase. For some reason it surprised me that grownups could run. Then the doors would open and one or two fire trucks would emerge with firemen clinging to the sides of the vehicles. The fire department tested the siren every noon using two cycles of up and down volume. Many people used the noon siren to set their clocks. The fire hall was also the police station. I think we had three or four cops at most, and they were mostly driving around town. I often walked home from school with a neighbor friend, and we would sneak a peek through the back door if it were left open. What impressed us was a lone prison cell. I don't think it was ever used in my lifetime, but it readily stimulated the imagination of a young boy.

Every summer we had a village festival. Some years we called it Farmer's Day; other years we called it Community Days. The main event was a carnival with a variety of rides. A Ferris wheel was the showpiece of each carnival, although they frequently had an octopus along with smaller rides for young kids. The rides were clustered at the east end of the main street. A double row of tents housing con-artists lined the west end of the street. We knew they were con-artists and not the most honest, but we were there to have fun. A variety of trinkets hung from the walls of their tents and was available to anyone who could knock down the heavily-weighted milk bottles or shoot a sufficient number of moving targets with a pellet gun.

Meanwhile, other activities were occurring at the Balyeat Field behind the movie theater. There was the customary water fight between our fire department and a neighboring fire department. Everyone including spectators was thoroughly drenched by the end of the contest. On a hot day in July, no one cared. This event was often followed by a trailer pulling contest where local farmers pulled trailers through a maze of pylons with their tractors. It didn't get tricky until they were required to back the trailer through the same maze. The most difficult feat was backing a trailer with a swiveling front axle. This allowed the trailer to buckle at both the tractor hitch and the swiveling front axle. It was amazing how well some of those farmers maneuvered their trailers in such short times.

As dusk settled over the festivities, flood lights illuminated Balyeat Field; it was time for the Merchants vs. Farmers softball game. Almost everyone fell into one of the two groups. There were few non-partisans. As the owner of the B & T Dairy, my father played on the Merchant Team for several years until he broke his thumb catching a ball. Despite the intense rivalry, it was a friendly game, and everyone shook hands with the opponents at the end of the game—unless your thumb was broken.

When the flood lights dimmed I knew we were in for a treat. This was my favorite part of the Community Days—fireworks! Today any fireworks display comes with trained technicians who personally monitor and ignite the explosive missiles. A system of electronics orchestrates the entire event. All that was unnecessary in the 1950s. A few local firemen with cigarette lighters were all that was needed. For the most part they had a good safety record, although one year the roof of a nearby house caught fire. The firemen quickly extinguished the blaze resulting in only minimal damage to the house. When multiple and simultaneous explosions of color flooded the sky, I knew it was the grand finale and the end of the festivities. It was also past my bedtime. Sometimes I was fast asleep before our car reached our driveway.

Some summers we had a circus. This was never an annual event, and we were excited when their arrival was announced in the paper. Circuses need large vacant areas to set up their tents. One such area was on the southern edge of town, well within walking or biking distance from our house. My parents were not fond of circuses, because they had once gone to a circus where a trapeze artist fell to her death. It was not a pleasant experience for them, and they did not wish to have us share a similar experience. In the early circus days no nets were used. It was thought that the added danger added to the athletic stunts done high in the air.

Even without admission to the big tent, there was quality entertainment to be had. The circus arrived in a caravan of large trucks. Some of the trucks housed wild animals such as lions and tigers. Other trucks housed tamer animals such as elephants. Every child and many adults showed up to watch them unload. This was part of the circus performance, and the players milked it for all it was worth. A good show while erecting the tent turned into ticket sales.

The main tent was too big and heavy to be carried in one piece, so several sections had to be strapped together with heavy cord. This was time consuming and not much of a spectator sport. We wanted to see the tent rise up, but we knew this would happen in a matter of seconds. We feared we would miss this event if we did not remain vigilant. I sometimes I think the performers delayed raising the tent until the waiting crowds could wait no longer.

We knew they were getting serious when the center poles were hoisted into a vertical position by one or more elephants. I am sure they could have achieved the same results with ropes attached to pickup trucks, but they were entertainers and masters of their craft. There were usually two or three center poles depending on the size of the tent. They were erected such that the base was lodged in an opening at the center of the tent. Ropes attached to the tent weaved their way through pulleys at the top of the poles. When all was ready, elephants pulled on the ropes and the tent rose within seconds to the top of the center pole. It was not unusual for the crowd of on-lookers to cheer when the canvas reached the top.

The excitement was over but not all the work. Every employee from ticket seller to lion tamer converged on the tent. The canvas was stretched out and side poles erected. Watching men and women attend to the final details was boring and much of the crowd dispersed. I am sure there was plenty of work being done inside the tent to make way for the first performance on the following afternoon.

Even though my parents would not take me to the circus, I did see several performances with groups like the cub scouts. As I remember, there was too much to see at once. They often had acts performing in two separate rings. As a lion tamer had his cats do tricks in one ring, trapeze artists were climbing to the top of the tent in another ring to prepare for their act. Watching them adjust their ropes and swings was as much fun as watching the lion tamer. While all this was going on, clowns walked in front of the bleachers doing funny tricks. And there were venders selling cotton candy, peanuts, and a wide assortment of items of wonder. One year I bought a chameleon, which is supposed to turn colors to match its environment. My mother was not pleased with this purchase as my brother and I had a couple of these small lizards wandering around the house. They were particularly attracted to curtains.

Most activities around Sparta were only of local interest. This was not so with the annual rodeo. This occurred every fall at Bettes' Hill located just west of town. I did not often attend, but if I remember right the spectators sat on the hillside to watch the event. The rodeo drew contestants from all around the nation and spectators came from neighboring states. Sparta was inundated with horses and riders. It was during a rodeo weekend that I saw my first Indian. He was standing on the corner of State and Division Streets fully dressed as a Plains Indian. I remember being very excited at the time. Many people in Sparta enjoyed the rodeo, but others considered it a nuisance. It did bring many undesirable characters into town, but it also brought in their money. For the most part, my family ignored the rodeo.

I have fond memories of Sparta in the fall. Sparta is an old town with many majestic maple trees. Each fall their leaves would turn yellow, red, or occasionally purple. The leaves immersed the streets in color, creating a beautiful sight. Eventually, the leaves fell to the ground and covered the grass. That made them even more enjoyable. I shuffled through the leaves just to hear the rustling noise.

There was more fun to be had once our parents raked the leaves into a large pile. Then my older brother and I could jump into the pile and disappear under the leaves. There were many air pockets, which allowed us to breath and the leaves above us were almost weightless. It was the 1950s' equivalent to today's tub filled with balls found at some McDonalds.

Eventually, residents needed to dispose of the leaves. Most residents raked their leaves to the curb and then set them on fire. Curbs had a 12-18 inch apron of non-flammable concrete that prevented the asphalt from catching fire. Leaves do not create a hot fire like firewood. They burn slowly and release lots of smoke. It was not uncommon to look down a side street and see six or more columns of smoke rising into the air. The smoke added a pleasant aroma to the fall air. We lived on the highway, and I don't remember burning leaves at the curb, but my older brother remembers people burning leaves on State St. He says the smoke on State St. was sometimes so thick that drivers turned on their headlights.

Fall was also reserved for football. The local football team not only represented Sparta High School; they represented the Sparta Township. When the team played at Balyeat Field behind the movie theater, most of the town gathered to root for the home team. My father was one of the fans. My older brother and I would often join him, but football should not be a spectator sport. We frequently organized our own football games in the open field behind the bleachers. Sometimes we had as many as eight to ten boys. We made up rules as we needed them. We paused periodically to check the score of the "Big Game" when shouting and applause from the bleachers became boisterous. My father seldom missed an away game and never missed a home game. He always took my older brother and me with him. It made for an exciting evening for all concerned.

We also played football during recess at school. I don't know who thought of the idea, but someone suggested playing football on Saturday mornings at Balyeat Field. Every boy in our grade was invited. Come Saturday morning there were about fifteen of us playing on the same field as the high school team. We had no helmets or shoulder pads, and this was tackle football. I think we had some abrasions, but no serious injuries. We played football every Saturday morning until it became too cold.

Visiting the local dump provided quality entertainment. It was located on the outskirts of town. We didn't have the environmental concerns that we have today. The dump was nothing more than a large ravine, and it was open twenty-four hours a day. People brought their junk and dumped it. When my brother and I went to the dump with my father, we often returned with more items than my father dumped. For a young child the dump was filled with hidden treasures. Sometimes we returned at night with a spotlight to watch the rats take over the dump. Once when I was a teenager, my grandfather and I went to the dump at night to shoot rats with a .22 caliber rifle. I seriously doubt this significantly reduced the population of rats.

8

Grand Rapids

Even though everything we would want could be purchased in Sparta or the Sears and Roebuck catalogue, it was a family tradition to visit that great metropolis to the south during the Christmas season. For an eight-year-old, visiting Grand Rapids was an overwhelming experience. I looked up at towering sky scrapers, some of which were twenty stories tall. The tallest sky scraper in Sparta at the time was two stories. I distinctly remember the streets were clogged with city busses that belched black smoke filled with sulfurous stench. I held my breath whenever they passed.

My parents were not interested in the skyscrapers; they were here to visit two department stores: Wurzburgs and Herpolsheimers. They weren't the tallest, but they were still massive. Wurzburgs offered ten large floors of merchandise. That is too many stairs for most people to climb. Fortunately,

they offered two carnival rides, at least that was how my older brother and I viewed them.

My favorite carnival ride was the escalator. Jack and I could ride half way up the escalator and turn around and walk down. It was like walking on a treadmill—we went nowhere. Shoppers trying to ride to the next floor were not impressed with our behavior, but we were having fun. You may be wondering where our parents were. They were busy with our two younger brothers. I am sure they watched out of the corner of their eye to ensure we did not get lost. We also kept an eye on them, so we were not left behind. Even free range children have responsibilities.

The other "carnival ride" was the elevator. This was not as much fun as the escalator because it was operated by a woman on a stool who had no intention of relinquishing control to two young boys. My parents would lead us into this box and tell the operator, "Fourth floor, please." The operator would pull a lever after the doors closed. I would feel the floor of the elevator push against my feet. The force must have been at least 1.1 g's. As the elevator worked its way to the fourth floor, I pondered the odds of the elevator cables breaking and the elevator crashing in the basement. I had a theory that I would be spared if I could time the fall of the elevator perfectly and jumped into the air just before the elevator crashed. Later in life when I studied physics I discovered that Newton had a different theory.

Elevator Chauffeur   Elevator Instrument Panel

As we approached the fourth floor, the elevator operator would pull back on her control lever. The force of gravity would diminish. It reminded me of being on a swing at the top of the arc where gravity reclaims control. The operator never stopped even with the floor. She would have to tweak the lever before she could open the door and announce, "Fourth floor, lingerie!"

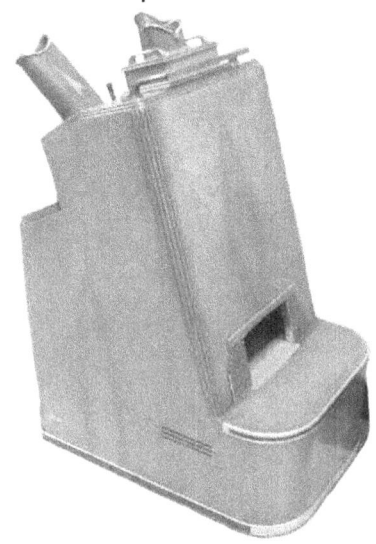

My favorite floor was footwear. They offered another "toy" for my brother and me to play with. It was called fluoroscopy, which provided continuous X-rays in a video format. While our parents were paying for our shoes, we were free to insert our shoes into the machine. It was quality entertainment watching our bones wiggle within the shoes.

X-rays were not considered dangerous in the '50s. The fluoroscopy machines disappeared from shoe stores in the mid-fifties because they were too expensive, and the novelty had worn off. I still have fond memories of the machines, as I wait for the cancer on my toes to develop.

Herpolsheimers had five floors, but each floor was huge and they rivaled Wurzburgs. They were famous for their animated Christmas display windows. We ran from one display to the next. There were displays of Santa and the elves working at the North Pole workshop, and displays of Santa flying over rooftops in his sleigh. Rudolf would turn his head to look at us and then give us a wink. To a young boy the animated objects appeared real.

Herpolsheimers had even more to offer in the humongous basement. A monorail train called the Santa Express ran around the perimeter of the basement, the store was that big. Herpolsheimers is now gone but the Santa Express can still be seen at the Grand Rapids Museum.

Santa Express

Ramona Park

Sparta offered a one-screen movie house and concerts in the park during the summer, but sometimes Spartans needed more. Ramona Park in E. Grand Rapids filled this void. Ramona Park opened to the public in 1897. Due to decreased business it was forced to close in 1955 when I was only nine. I was too young for many of the rides, but they were still fun to watch. The cynosure of the park was the Jack Rabbit Derby Racer, which was a double wooden-track roller coaster with an eighty percent drop. Straight down was ninety percent. I could hear the screams throughout the park as the roller coaster plunged over the top of summit. It looked and sounded terrifying. I couldn't wait until I was old enough to take a ride on the Jack Rabbit or the more tranquil Ferris Wheel. Unfortunately, the park closed before I reached that magical age. I was limited to the age-appropriate Merry-go-round and the small cars that followed a

well-defined circular path. We did not scream like the people on the roller coaster, but we still had a lot of fun.

There were some rides that people of all ages enjoyed. One of them was a narrow-gauge steam locomotive that pulled several passenger cars a half mile around the perimeter of the park. It created a lot of smoke and steam, and its whistle could be heard throughout the park. In its heyday it carried as many as 50,000 people a year.

Ramona Park also operated a boat livery on Reeds Lake, where small skiffs could be rented for a modest fee. For individuals wanting something more substantial, there was the SS Ramona. The Ramona was a steamboat that sailed the lake between 1923 and 1954.

One summer our family went to Ramona Park with the intention of having a picnic onboard the Ramona. The Ramona provided picnic tables onboard for such occasions. My father paid the fare while my mother spread our feast on a table cloth we brought to cover the bird-stained picnic table. We were enjoying the good food and scenery as the boat cruised along the shore, but we had not finished eating when the boat returned to the dock. My father was not happy with such a short trip. He went to the gangplank to purchase tickets for another tour around the lake. He returned with a big smile; we were free to ride as long as we wanted with one ticket. We made several enjoyable trips around the lake and got our money's worth. In 1956, the ship was scrapped and burned. Ramona Park was no more.

Home

I spent my childhood from birth to high school graduation at 226 S. State St. We called it State Street, but it was also M-37, which was a very busy north-south corridor heading north from Grand Rapids. Fortunately, our house was on the east side of the highway. That was where most of the kids my age lived, so I seldom crossed the highway.

I didn't realize it at the time, but it was a very small house with small rooms. Perhaps I didn't notice because I was also small. The house had three bedrooms, two of which were upstairs. The ceilings on these bedrooms sloped downward on both sides, making parts of the rooms challenging for my father who was six feet two inches. Closet space was carved out of the bedroom where the slope of the ceiling was too low for other practical use.

We had one bathroom and that was located on the ground floor in an inconvenient location. Anyone wishing to use the facility had to walk through the downstairs bedroom. There was no tub, only a shower that was in need of repair. I occasionally showered with my father when I was very small, but most of the time I took a bath in an old washtub that my mother placed in the shower for that purpose. When you are small, a washtub is as much fun as a hot tub.

In the front of the house was an unheated enclosed porch, where we stored boots, coats, and wet umbrellas. Another door led into a small dining room. A living room of similar size was to the right of the dining room. Later, the partition between the two rooms was removed to provide one large dining/living room.

Progressing past the dining room led into the modest kitchen and then into the unheated back porch. We used the back porch in a similar fashion as the front porch. If all the doors were open, it was possible to see through the front door all the way through the back door. Even though it was a small house, my parents were young and they made it a home.

A door just off from the kitchen led to our basement. I don't know why, but I feared the basement. The stairs had no railing, and there were no risers to the steps. In my youthful imagination, I feared I might slip between the steps. I knew this was impossible, but I feared it just the same. It was also possible a gremlin could grab my ankles as I descended the stairs. Once I reached the bottom of the stairs, I was fine.

There was not much to see at the bottom of the stairs. The ceiling was too low for any living quarters, and the walls leaked after a good rain. In some areas, the wet soil had pushed the blocks inward. My father stored tools such as hammers and screwdrivers in the basement, but the major reason for visiting the basement was to stoke the furnace. Our entire house was heated by coal.

Every morning my father would get up and add coal to the furnace. There was a damper to control the heat similar to a potbelly stove, but for the most part my father's arms were the thermostat. Sometimes he would come home in the afternoon to add more coal. It was a burdensome job, and if the fire ever went out, it was difficult to restart. Coal burns as readily as charcoal, and he did not have charcoal lighter fluid.

We stored the coal in a coal bin under the front porch. Every fall a dump truck filled with coal showed up in our driveway. A metal chute was inserted through a basement window and the coal was unloaded into the coal bin. It was a fascinating spectacle to watch when you are a young boy with nothing better to do.

You could say we had central heat, because the heat from our coal furnace went straight up to a grill in the center of the living room/dining room. The rest of the house received heat by convection. This made a cold kitchen and a hot living room. The heating grill sometimes became so hot it could cause burns. My mother warned us of those times, and we then knew enough to walk around the grill. When the grill was not hot, it was a fun place to insert marbles and listen to them roll down the ductwork. I don't know if this harmed the furnace, but it did not make my parents happy.

We had no heating ducts in the upstairs, but fortunately, heat rises, and the stairs leading to the second level were open. If the bedroom doors were open, a significant amount of heat reached the rooms. That did not mean the bedrooms were toasty-warm. I remember many cold nights when I had to slip between cold sheets and shiver. My parents advised me that it would warm up, but it often took five minutes before my body heat warmed the sheets. It seemed like forever to a young shivering child. We had plenty of blankets, so we slept well for the rest of the night.

The basement was also home to the fuse box. Circuit breakers had yet to be invented. Every time I placed two wires into a wall socket sparks would fly and the power would go out. (I was an inquisitive child.) My father would then go into the basement and replace the fuse. He kept extra fuses on hand. I am not sure if I was the reason for the extra fuses or not. There were some people who inserted a penny between the fuse and the fuse box. This would bypass the fuse and re-electrify the circuit. This was not a safe practice, and I don't think my father ever did that.

We had little need for electricity other than for lighting, refrigerator, and range. My mother had a washing machine but no dryer. She hung wet clothing outside on a clothesline—even in the winter. Permanent press clothes had yet to be invented, and my mother ironed clothes by hand. Since steam irons were unavailable, my mother sprinkled water on the clothes using a coke bottle caped with cork and a sprinkler head. Washing, drying, ironing, and folding clothing took most of the day for a large family.

We had a phone. Many families did not. We were on a party line with the B & T Dairy. Our phone number was 4873 and the B & T Dairy's phone number was 4871. That provides a prospective of how small Sparta was. Anything beyond four digits was long distance. Before anyone made a call, it was necessary to pick up the phone and listen. If someone was using the phone at the dairy, the phone was returned to the cradle. Proper etiquette required waiting a few minutes before trying again.

Some party lines had four or more phone customers, and they did not always follow proper etiquette. It was not uncommon for a nosey individual to listen in on conversations. If this was suspected all that was needed was a firm, "Mable, get off the line!" Each member of the party line had a distinctive ring. Our ring was a short ring followed by a long ring and the B & T Dairy was two long rings.

Long distance calling was very expensive and seldom used unless someone died or there was a birth in the family. Before placing a long distance call the intended message was written down—the phone companies charged by the minute. There were three ways to make a long distance call: a collect call where the answering individual accepted and paid for the call, a person to person call where the caller asked for a particular person (the operator would ask for this person before connecting the call), and a regular long distance call. I don't think my parents ever participated, but there was a scam where someone would call person to person and ask for Mr. Brian Boy. The person at the other end would tell the operator that Brian was not available. No phone charges were incurred and the receiving party knew that the baby was a boy named Brian.

We only had rotary phones. There were no buttons to push, no programmed phone numbers or speed dial. To dial a six, the caller lifted the speaker, listened for the dial tone to insure no one on the party line was using the phone, and then inserted the index finger into the loop above the number six. The caller rotated the finger clockwise around the dial until the finger hit a finger guard. Dialing one rotated the dial a small distance, while the six dialed a much larger distance. When the finger was removed, the dial returned to its previous position while sending six clicks into the phone line. It was these series of clicks that connected the caller to the correct person.

This did not work for long distance. Long distance required additional help. Dialing zero or "O" for operator connected the caller to a real person. If you did not know the number of the person you were calling, no problem; the helpful lady looked up the number from the individual's name and address. The operator sat in front of a large switchboard with many cables and plugs. If the caller wished to talk to a friend in New York, the operator would plug in a cable connecting to a New York operator, who would plug in a cable to the desired person. Sometimes many operators were involved, which was the reason for the high cost of long distance calls.

The small house became even smaller with the arrival of two younger siblings. My father was not rich, but he must have been doing well enough to renovate the house. It helped that my grandfather was willing to design and do most of the work. My father could follow directions, but he was not a carpenter.

I think the first renovation was converting the back porch into a small eating area adjacent to the kitchen. We almost never used the formal dining room. When the opening into the living room was enlarged, the formal dining room became annexed.

I was too young to be of any help, but I was a good go-fer for my grandfather. I was also an intensive spectator. The renovation included a new entrance to our only bathroom. The worn out and deteriorating shower was replaced by a more respectable shower.

There were no plastic pipes at that time. The toilet was connected to the sewer with sections of cast iron. I found the way my grandfather sealed the segments most interesting. One end of each segment was flared out to accommodate the next section, but that did not make the connection watertight. My grandfather packed the area around the connection with oakum, which was twisted hemp impregnated with tar. Then he would seal it with hot lead. He melted the lead with a blow torch that ran on kerosene. A small thumb pump at the bottom of the blow torch provided pressure for the "blow" part of the blow torch. A special attachment on the top of the blow torch held a cast iron cup with a long handle just in front of the flame. My grandfather placed small chunks of solid lead into the cup. I was mesmerized as I watched the lead melt. When my grandfather thought it was sufficiently hot, he would pour it over the oakum to seal the sewer pipes. Some of the lead dripped down forming lead icicles as they hardened. These were returned to the cast iron cup for recycling.

My grandfather always left some of the lead icicles for me to play with. Freshly melted lead is shiny and malleable. I was able to bend and twist the lead strips into interesting figures. We used no gloves and did not worry about washing hands. Lead poisoning was not considered a high risk. Our exposure was limited to a short time period in our lives.

One of the greatest innovations, at least in my father's opinion, had little to do with my lifestyle. We still had a coal furnace, which my father frequently had to stoke. Sometimes he came home during the day to add coal to the furnace. I am sure my mother also assisted in this chore. Then my father purchased a state of the art, automatic stoker. It consisted of a large metal box that my father filled with coal. A small conveyor belt slowly fed coal from the coal box into the furnace. A speed control functioned as our thermostat. We still had uneven heating throughout the house, but for my father it meant fewer trips to the basement and that was paradise. Eventually, natural gas became available and the coal furnace was sent to the junk yard. It had served us faithfully for many years, but progress always wins out. With the gas furnace we were able to control the house temperature with a real thermostat. Two heat ducts at the ends of the living room replaced the dangerous grill in the center of the floor. There was no heat in the kitchen or upstairs.

Heating the house still relied on convection, which left many cold areas.

With no further need of coal, we had an empty coal bin under the front porch. On April 3rd, 1956 a tornado struck Standale, killing seventeen people. This created an irrational fear for my mother, so my father turned the coal bin into a storm shelter. It was isolated from the rest of the basement and had three cinderblock walls. He stretched large pipes across the ceiling and covered them with cardboard to catch any falling debris. My mother found an old bed to add to the shelter. I don't know how she envisioned six people sleeping on the bed during a major storm, but it made a nice play room.

My older brother and I slept in an upstairs bedroom. We were young and our parents did not want us walking down the stairs in the middle of the night to use the bathroom. Their solution was a large coffee can, which became our urinal during the night. We seldom used it, but at times it was invaluable.

Renovation and reconstruction on our house continued. One day I looked up the stairs toward our bedrooms and saw clouds floating by. That was not supposed to be. I climbed to the top of the steps to investigate. Normally, there were two bedrooms, one on either side of the landing, but what I found were the two bedrooms and a giant hole in the wall between them. My grandfather was in the process of creating a dormer. We would soon have an upstairs bathroom with a real shower and tub. No more coffee-can urinals. Our house was growing.

The biggest addition was a recreation room at the back of the house. My brother and I were older by then and actually helped with the construction. My brother lacked basic carpentry skills. You could always tell which nails he pounded in—they were surrounded by hammer marks. I was impressed with the flooring. My father and grandfather laid a four-inch thick layer of cement mixed with a granular insulation. When it was dry we could walk on it, but it was not as strong as concrete. They laid loops of copper pipe on top of this and then covered it with concrete. A water heater pumped hot water through the coils to heat the floor. It was the only heat in the house outside of the two registers in the front room. The warm floor felt so good on bare feet. We had a cat at that time, and we could always tell where a pipe was—it was under the cat. The new addition was added about the time that my father sold the B & T Dairy. He salvaged the grill from the dairy and added it to the corner of the room. We often used it to fry hamburgers or make pancakes for large parties. The B & T Dairy had been a big part of my father's life. I think he secretly enjoyed keeping a piece of the dairy.

Once all the children flew the coop, my mother wanted to move into a small condominium. It was hard for my father at first. The house was also a home and had many memories. It has since been razed and is now a parking lot for a gas station and convenience store.

10

Free Range Children

I don't know if the world was less dangerous when I was growing up, but we did worry less. We did not have instant news. What happened in California stayed in California. If there were a serial killer in Georgia, it was unlikely to headline in the *Grand Rapids Press*. My parents raised their children as if we lived in a safe and carefree world. Sociologists now have a name for it. It is called free range children and was the norm when I was growing up. It is not that helicopter parents did not exist, but they were an exception. My mother had a cousin who was raised by helicopter parents. My mother always felt sorry for her, since she missed out in so much fun.

Today free range parenting is almost outlawed. In some areas children cannot walk to a park without adult supervision. Leaving a child alone at home depends on age and not maturity of the child. The jury is still out as to which method produces better children. There is probably more safety with helicopter parenting, but there are studies that suggest free range children become more mature and independent. One thing is for sure— we had more fun growing up.

I don't remember much of my toddler years. My first more than fleeting memories were at age five or six. I was allowed to play outside without supervision, but I am sure there was an adult in the house who often looked out at me. If I were playing with my older brother, there was less concern. I did not have a formal sandbox with a wooden frame. Instead, my father dug a one foot deep hole in the shape of a square and filled it with beach sand. I remember playing in this sand box for many days in the summer. My parents assumed I would stay in our yard, which I did. I was as likely to be barefoot and shirtless as not. This dress attire would be common for several years to come. My mother probably thought this created fewer clothes to wash.

As I got older my horizon grew. There was a great world beyond my yard. I was fortunate to live in a neighborhood with eight boys on the northwest corner of our block—they all lived within a two-hundred yard radius with no streets to cross. We did have two girls, but they seldom joined our activities. Play dates were unheard of, and we seldom played inside someone's house. On any given summer day our parents pushed us out the door, and we were eager to go. Other parents did the same. It didn't take long before we were organized and group games began. Softball was always popular. We played in a vacant lot my parents purchased. They placed a chicken-wire fence around the lot to protect the neighboring buildings. We didn't have enough people for teams, so we normally played what we called "work-up." When the batter was out, the pitcher became a batter and the first baseman became pitcher. Everyone moved up a position. We played until it was too dark to see or our parents called us to come home. We didn't have cell phones. When our parents wanted us home for supper or bedtime, they would go to the back door and yell our names. All the parents did that. It was not considered unusual.

Another popular game was "kick the can." The person who was "it" would place a foot on a can and count to thirty while everyone hid. When the person who was "it" found someone, he would run back to the can, place a foot on the can, and say, "one, two, three on Jack." The person who was found would have to stand near the can. If someone could sneak in and kick the can, everyone was free and scattered. It was a simple game, but it kept us occupied.

Sometime during the spring or summer, pea-shooter season began. We had no control over the timing, but it was an annual event determined by the local Ben Franklin store. Pea shooters showed up on the shelves and we bought them. They were nothing more than simple plastic tubes. We bought peas, beans, or sometimes popcorn from the corner convenience store. It required a bit of skill, but with a mouthful of peas, beans, or popcorn, we could blow them through the tube one at a time. War was on. No one was safe except for parents. We knew better than to shoot at them. Several weeks later it was not unusual to find beans and corn growing freely throughout the neighborhood. One summer a star of a Saturday children's show visited a relative in Sparta. We all went over to get autographs. A photographer from the *Grand Rapids Press* also showed up in time to take a picture of my younger brother Bob—shirtless with a pea shooter in his back pocket.

The size of my world took a quantum leap when I got a bicycle. Bicycles came in two colors: blue for girls and red for boys. That may seem to be a strange color code, but no boy with any self-esteem would ride any other color. The girls' bikes also lacked a crossbar in case they were wearing a dress or skirt. Sometimes we would attach a playing card or a balloon to the spokes with clothespins to add noise. We then envisioned we rode motorcycles.

With a bicycle I was no longer confined to my neighborhood. Now the entire town and much of the countryside was my domain. As long as I showed up for meals and bedtime, my parents didn't care. I could pedal to Rogue River to fish, head over to Balyeat Field to play football or just ride to feel the wind in my face. One day John Badgerow and I pedaled down to the sewage plant. The plant had several sprinklers with arms like an octopus. The legs of this octopus sprayed water over a bed of rocks as it slowly revolved around its axis. With nothing better to do John and I rode one of the arms like a merry-go-round, being careful not to fall onto the wet rocks. Free range kids definitely had more fun.

11

Automobiles

I was not born in the horse and buggy era like my grandfather, but our cars were still primitive. There was a Ford dealership next door to the B & T Dairy Bar, which was where my father purchased his cars. He believed in patronizing his friends, and the owner of the dealership took his coffee breaks at the B & T.

My father once had a pickup truck, but the earliest car I remember was a convertible. It must have been around 1950, since my brother Bob was an infant. He was not popular, because my mother proclaimed it was too cold for him with the top down. We were excited whenever we went somewhere with another family. Then we could stuff Mom and Bob in the other car, and my father could be the hero and drive all the kids with the top down. Convertibles were nice in the summer, but the cloth top provided little insulation in the winter.

Cars in the 1950s were not reliable. Tires frequently blew out, and on a hot summer day it was not uncommon for car engines to overheat. Steam would ooze out from under the hood. When this happened, my father pulled off the road and lifted the hood. The radiator caps must have had a pressure-release valve, because that was always the source of the steam. My father used a rag to remove the radiator cap, doing his best to avoid burns from the hot steam. The boiling water gushed up like Old Faithful in miniature. If we were lucky, we would have water in the car to replace the water that had boiled out, otherwise my father hiked to the nearest stream or farmhouse. My father slowly added the water to the radiator while the engine was running. Otherwise, the sudden input of cold water would crack the engine block. If it were a particularly hot day and my father was worried about the car overheating, he turned on the heater. This helped draw heat from the engine and prevented overheating, but it was not pleasant for those riding in the car. We rolled down the windows and did the best we could with a bad situation.

Early cars lacked automatic chokes. Starting a car was similar to starting a lawn mower. Pulling out a knob to the right of the steering wheel opened the choke. Once the engine turned over, the choke was slowly pushed back in. My mother forgot to push it in on several occasions, which flooded the engine. We had to wait several minutes before restarting the car. Cars now have automatic chokes, which makes starting a car less complicated.

The life expectancy of a car was about 100,000 miles after which the engine was no longer considered reliable. About the same time most cars in the northern states had large rusted-out holes in the frame. I once had a Ford Mustang with a floor so rusty that the driver's seat broke loose. Southern cars fared better, but the salty roads of winter took its toll on northern cars. When my parents' car's odometer reached the magical 100,000 miles, we knew we would soon see a new (used) car.

I can only remember one time that my father bought a new car. That was a Ford station wagon. We were now a family of six and needed the extra room. New cars were not purchased off the lot like they are today; they were special ordered. The dealership usually had a few demo cars to show the virtues of the new car. Colors were chosen from a brochure. After considerable debate, my parents decided to go with silver mocha and colonial white. Cars with two colors were standard at the time.

Cars in the 1950s were more spacious. The front seat was a full-width, bench seat large enough for three adults. The person in the middle had less leg room due to the hump housing the transmission. The gear shifter was attached to the right side of the steering wheel, which provided more room for the middle passenger. Even so, it was considered proper etiquette for a girlfriend to sit in the middle next to her beau. On long, late-night trips, my brother often slept stretched out on the back seat while I slept in the front with my head on my mother's lap and my feet on my father's lap. We didn't worry about seatbelts; they weren't invented yet.

I have many fond memories of that station wagon. We once took a trip to Yellowstone. My grandfather built a box for the top of the car. We filled this with our tent and sleeping bags, which left the interior of the car empty. Sometimes we would recline the backseat, which left a large area for playing card games or other similar activities. No one cared where we sat in the car. We survived quite nicely without seatbelts.

We could have driven through Chicago to get to Yellowstone, but there was a new modern-day miracle to be seen at the Straits of Mackinac. The two Michigan peninsulas are separated by five miles of water. Prior to 1957, the only way to reach the Upper Peninsula was by a ferry such as Vacationland. In the summer of 1957 the Mackinac Bridge open to autos and trucks for the first time.

Vacationland

Early cars lacked many of today's amenities. Radios were a luxury and came at an additional charge. Our radios were limited to a.m. stations. FM stations were another luxury not available in the 1950s. The radio was connected to a whip antenna located on the car's right front fender. It was not uncommon to fly a fox or squirrel's tail from the top of the antenna.

We had no power steering or power brakes. If you wanted to roll down your window, you rolled it down with a hand crank. Unless there were other people in the car, adjusting other windows required pulling off to the side of the road. Every car had a useless clock. They never seemed to work. Most clocks were mounted on the glove compartment door. They were wind-up clocks. Some of them had alarms, but I could never figure out why an alarm clock was needed while driving. Even if someone opened the glove box door and wound the clocks daily, they seldom kept accurate time.

Most cars in the 50s were stick shift with a clutch in addition to the brake and gas pedal. When I took driver's training in the summer of 1962, about half of all automobiles still had stick shifts. Automatic transmissions were becoming popular, but this added to the cost of the car. I learned to drive on a car with a stick shift located on the right side of the steering wheel. We learned to drive through a high school program, and they felt if you learned how to drive a stick shift, you could drive any car. This proved to be a valuable skill when I drove 2 ½ ton trucks in Vietnam.

There was another advantage to the stick shift. If a driver left the lights on or the battery became uncharged, it was possible to start the engine by pushing the car until it was rolling at five or ten miles an hour. Then the driver released the clutch and engaged the first gear. This was often enough to turn the engine over and start the car. I can remember many times pushing a car to get it started. If several strong men were unavailable to push a car, another vehicle often gave the helpless car a push. Early cars had real bumpers made of steel and rubber in the front and rear of the car, which made this possible. Bumpers are now non-existent. They have been replaced by fragile plastic. The slightest bump can create thousands of dollars of damage.

Turn signals were non-existent in the fifties. If a driver wanted to turn left, he rolled down his window and extended his arm toward the left. That gesture was universal among the states, but Michigan had additional signals for right turns and stops. An outstretched arm with the forearm bent up at the elbow signified a right turn and a similar gesture with the forearm extending downward signified slowing down or stopping. Needless to say, many people did not use hand signals. During Michigan's cold winters, the manual turn signals were almost non-existent.

The ubiquitous gas station with convenience store had yet to make its appearance. We had service stations. My father would pull up to a gas pump and an energetic man would rush out to his window. The price of gas in 1950 was about $0.27 per gallon, which would be about $2.94 in 2020 dollars. My father would often tell the attendant to give him a couple of dollars' worth or fill it up. While the gas was filling the tank, the attendant checked the pressure in the tires and washed the windows. He still wasn't done. The attendant lifted the hood and checked the oil level. It was not uncommon for the attendant to bring the dipstick to the driver's window as proof of adequate oil level. There was not much of interest inside the store. They sold fuses, oil, maps and windshield wipers, but no food other than perhaps a rack of candy bars. Instead, there was frequently a couple of car lifts for changing oil and tires. The service station owner could make more money changing oil that he could selling a bag of chips.

Nothing was more luxurious in the 60s than air conditioning. It was only found in the wealthiest homes. Perhaps it was more common in the Deep South where summers were longer and hotter. No one was more surprised than I was when Bill DeHart, our school superintendent, drove up to the Tastee Treat where I was working during the summer of 1964. I was on break when his wife called me over to their car. She had been my sixth-grade teacher. It was a hot summer day, and I was sweating. She invited me to sit in the back seat of their car. It was like entering a walk-in cooler. I could have sat there all afternoon if I didn't need to return to work. I was not aware that air conditioning could fit in a car. Household air conditioners were rather large. Mrs. DeHart was almost apologetic as she explained they needed the air conditioner because of her husband's heart condition. Now every car has air conditioning even if the owner is in excellent health.

Air conditioning was the first of many luxuries now considered standard features in new cars. We have reclining heated seats, safety air bags, built-in video players for back-seat passengers, surround cameras to assist backing up, satellite radio, and automatic braking in case the driver's reactions are slow. What's next; a car that drives itself?

It was almost unheard of for a family to have more than one car. People had places to go, and one car was not always sufficient. Fortunately, we had thumbs. Hitchhiking was a respectable form of transportation, and we didn't have to stand very long on the road with our thumb out before someone would stop to offer a ride. That was just the friendly thing to do. We had no fear of encountering a psychopath.

12

Elementary School

There was no such thing as preschool in the 1950s. When I was five years old, my parents enrolled me in kindergarten. Since there was no bussing inside the village, my parents were expected to provide transportation to school. Fortunately, John Badgerow who lived two doors down from our house was also beginning kindergarten. My father drove both of us to school, and John's father gave us a ride home. Kindergarten was only a half day, so I don't think I learned much more than the alphabet, numbers, and colors, but we had plenty of play time. I think the goal was to teach us how to socialize in a large group. Real education did not begin until first grade.

Once we graduated to first grade, we had two twenty-minute recesses, one in the morning and one in the afternoon. We had a playground with teeter-totters, slides, monkey bars, and a merry-go-round. Today most of these are considered too dangerous. I don't remember anyone receiving serious injuries on the playground. We always had minor cuts and abrasions. They were treated with Mercurochrome and Band-Aids by the teacher. People would have thought it strange to have a school nurse.

In the later elementary grades our recess time became more organized. Sometimes we would play crack the whip. We would join hands, and the lead person would start running in a small circle. Individuals at the far end were swung around at a very fast rate. Usually, it was faster than they could run, and they would fall down. Another popular game was "horseback." We would pair up with one person the horse and the partner was the rider. The object was to knock over the other teams. This game was highly competitive. Since I was bigger than most of my classmates, I was usually the horse. These were boys' games. I don't remember what girls did during recess, and as a fourth grader I didn't care.

In the winter it wasn't unusual to have snowball fights with dozens of kids on each side. If you got hit in the face, it did no good to cry to the teacher on duty. You were told if you didn't want to get hit in the face, you should stay away from the snowball area.

Every spring was marble season. This was also determined by the local Ben Franklin Store. When we saw marbles on the shelves, we knew it was marble season. Marbles came in two sizes. The regular marbles had the diameter of a dime. There were also larger marbles, which were about the diameter of a quarter. The playground at the school was covered with eight inches of pea gravel. To play marbles we would dig a small circular pit in the gravel or a semi-circle against the wall of a building. We would draw a well-defined edge with a finger to provide a border to the pit. Two people would begin the game by tossing marbles toward the pit from a predetermined line. If the marble landed inside the pit it was the next person's turn. This would continue until one of the players missed. If the opponent also missed there was no fault. If the opponent placed his marble inside the pit, all the marbles were his. Sometimes a player would declare dibs and throw one of the larger marbles. If he lost the marbles, he was allowed to replace the larger marble with a smaller marble.

School was not all fun and games. Teachers expected us to learn something. We had two classes for each grade with about twenty-five students in each class. There were no teachers' aides or outside help. The teacher was on her own. Sometimes we had a music teacher who came once a week to teach us how to sing. In late fall or early winter we learned Christmas carols. Religion was not pushed, but it also was not forbidden. I think I learned more about Hinduism, Islam, and Buddhism in our history and geography classes than I did about Christianity. Some students received special help from a speech pathologist. Stuttering was a common problem. I seldom hear anyone stuttering today. I assume it is corrected before students start school.

Not only did the teacher not have an aide, she also had to make her own copies for tests or handouts, and she didn't have a copy machine. When I was in early elementary the teacher used a gel the size of a sheet of paper. Somehow she transferred ink to the gel. Then she could press papers against the gel one at a time to make copies. I remember I enjoyed the smell of the paper copies. By the time I reached the upper elementary grades, the ink and gel were replaced by mimeograph machines. A lesson or test was typed onto a stencil that was later attached to the drum of the mimeograph machine. A hand crank rotated the drum to produce multiple copies.

We learned to read using the *Dick and Jane* series of books. The series was named after the main two characters. There was also a younger sister named Sally and a dog named Spot. These books were used in English speaking countries for over four decades. In the 1950s eighty percent of first-graders in the U.S. were using the series. They faded from classrooms in the 70s and 80s. Many people thought the characters were too white and too middle class.

At noon we were dismissed for an hour and a half. Students who lived close to the school walked home for lunch. The other students had metal lunch boxes. The boxes were highly decorated with cartoon characters such as Tinkerbell or Mickey Mouse. A few students brown-bagged it, but this was rare. There were no refrigerators. The students stored their lunches in their locker until noon. This would be unacceptable by today's health standards, but no one got sick.

Home was too far for me to walk in the allotted time, but the B & T Dairy was only ten minutes away. Many other students ate lunch at the B & T. It was always crowded. I ate in the office to avoid taking up counter space. Lunch consisted of cheeseburgers and chips, but I never tired of the menu.

Sometimes when one of the students had a birthday or it was a holiday, a parent would send cupcakes or cookies to school. These were always homemade. No respectable mother would send store-bought goodies, and no one ever got sick. Today homemade food products are banned by the health department.

I was expected to walk home after school. I usually walked home with John Badgerow who was in the same grade and lived two doors from our house. Our first stop was Phoebe's corner store. To a young child she looked like she was over one hundred years old. She had gray hair that was always tied up in a bun and wore wire-rim glasses. I remember her as a very nice lady who liked children. She lived by herself above the store. It was unheard of for a child to address an adult by first name. Phoebe was an exception. She was Phoebe and the name of her store was Phoebe's. If she had a last name, I never knew it. Her store offered every kind of candy and sugary treat. John and I usually bought a couple of large pretzels. We did not eat them right away, but saved them until we arrived behind the local Baptist Church. They had the biggest spruce tree in the world, and the tree had branches close to the ground. We would climb to the top of the tree, which was also the top of the world. Then we would sit and eat our pretzels. We were in no hurry to get home. We were free-range kids, and our parents were not concerned unless we were not home in time for dinner.

Some days instead of going to our climbing tree we would make a detour to Nash Creek. We chased frogs and tried to catch crawfish. The river always had something to offer for entertainment. We tried to avoid getting wet. We were free-range kids, but our parents did have limitations. There was a large concrete culvert in Rodger's Park that emptied into Nash Creek. Most of the time it was dry, but during a heavy rain it filled with drain water. I don't know if it was my idea or John's, but we decided we needed to know where it went. We climbed into the tube. We were small, but the tube was also small. Most of the time we had to crawl. If we had been smart or prepared we would have brought a flashlight. We were not prepared and our IQ was in question. As we crawled through the tube it began to get dark. It was one of those situations where neither one of us wanted to be the first one to admit fear. I wondered what would happen if the tunnel were to cave in or a sudden rainstorm were to develop. They were not pleasant thoughts. We crawled on. Eventually we turned a corner and could see a white speck in the distance. It appeared no larger than a bright star, but it was our light at the end of the tunnel. We crawled on. It finally opened into a small ravine more than two hundred yards from our starting point. We were wet and dirty, but we felt like we had climbed Mount Everest.

My greatest accomplishment in elementary school was learning how to read. They didn't warn me that it could be addicting. I remember my grandmother reading to me when I came to visit. She always had a stack of children's books she obtained from the library. I still remember some of the books. One book was about a steam shovel that helped build a sky scraper. The construction workers forgot about the steam shovel, and it became trapped within the building. When it looked like it was the end for the steam shovel, someone suggested they use the steam shovel's boiler to heat the building. The steam shovel lived happily ever after.

I can't recall my parents reading to us. I am not even sure if they had a library card. The first novel I remember my mother reading was a novel I wrote. My parents didn't have time for large chucks of reading, but they did read. My father read the newspaper every evening. He also read the *Reader's Digest* every month. My mother read *Better Homes and Gardens*. I also remember the *Saturday Evening Post*. They had the best cover pictures. My parents taught me by example that words on paper were important.

My three brothers shared my addiction for reading. Today kids sit around the breakfast table staring at their phones. We ate breakfast with spoon in one hand and cereal box in the other hand. We read our cereal boxes from cover to cover. It drove my mother crazy. Cereal boxes were quality reading in the fifties. Some had fun facts and others had puzzles. Most boxes came with a game or other trinket. This was always on the bottom of the box. We quickly learned to open the cereal box from the bottom. My mother was not happy with this either. Whoever got there first got to keep the toy.

One day Badgerow's corner store caught fire. There was considerable interior damage, and they had to discard all their cereal boxes. The neighborhood kids discovered them in a large dumpster. We ransacked the dumpster looking for the prizes in the cereal boxes. It was almost like Christmas in the summer.

I don't know how old I was when I got my first library card. Perhaps it was part of a field trip from school. It was not a long walk. My older brother had a library card, so it was not a new concept. Some teachers expected us to read a half hour in the afternoon. Personally, I think they just wanted a break and that was fine with me. The school didn't have a library, so the township library was our source of books.

I walked past the library every day on my way home from school. It was a formidable looking brick building that appeared intimidating from the outside. Inside was nothing more than a large room—but it was filled with books. It held row after row of bookshelves filled with books. The bookshelves reached almost to the ceiling. I could not reach those books even if I wanted to, but I was shorter in those days. Fortunately, the children's books were closer to the floor.

If anyone was looking for a particular book, they could find it in the card catalogue. The card catalogue was a wooden cabinet with many small drawers. The drawers held 3X5 cards describing each book. I never learned how to use the card catalogue. I didn't need to. I had my own private card catalogue. It was the librarian who sat at a large disk. She could find a book faster than anyone searching through those 3X5 cards. I think she had every book in the library memorized. She could look you straight in the eye and tell you exactly which book you needed to read.

One day the librarian introduced me to the *Black Stallion* by Walter Farley. It was about a young boy who was shipwrecked along with a mysterious black stallion. Alec Ramsay hung onto the black stallion, and the black stallion dragged him to a deserted island. When they were rescued, no one claimed the black stallion; it now belonged to Alec.

I was hooked. I always wanted a pony, but that was not an option for someone living in a city. When I read the *Black Stallion*, I became Alec and the horse was mine. We had a great adventure. I returned the book and told the librarian that I really enjoyed the book. She said Walter Farley had written other books about Alec and the Black Stallion. She led me to one of the stacks of books that didn't reach almost to the ceiling. She explained that this was the children's section. She pointed to a section under an F. There must have been over twenty books with Farley on the spine—and they were all about horses. I vowed to read every one of them.

If my memory is correct, I reached my goal. The librarian suggested other books that would be of interest, but I would have nothing to do with them. I wanted my Walter Farley novels. Later as an adult I wrote *The Song of Minnehaha*, which is a short story paying tribute to the Sparta Carnegie Library and their wonderful staff of librarians. It has been published in the *U.P. Reader #1* as well as the *Huffington Post*.

13

The Song of Minnehaha

A short story tribute to the Sparta Carnegie Library and their staff. Readers may skip to the next chapter to continue the biography.

"Sean, I got up early and went to town for groceries. I'll be back by noon. There's a breakfast burrito in the freezer. Nuke it for two minutes. And don't forget your insulin, ten units of regular and twenty of Lente."

Never marry a nurse; they always treat you like a patient. I've been taking insulin for twenty years. One would think that would suggest a modicum of medical knowledge. Despite her occasional nagging, Clara has been a good wife. I write "I'll be at my spot in the woods when you return" at the bottom of Clara's note and leave it on the kitchen table. My penmanship has never been great; now, with the arthritis in my hands, it is barely legible.

I walk over to the fridge and remove the vial of regular insulin; I won't need the Lente today. The breakfast burrito also does not fit my plans. I place the insulin and a syringe in a plastic grocery bag and head for the den.

We've been spending summers in this log cabin overlooking Lake Superior for thirty years. It is no longer a second home; for me, it is home. This is where I found motivation to write. Some of my best works owe their conception to a small spark of inspiration gleaned from these forty acres of Upper Peninsula wilderness.

Most of the cabin belongs to Clara, but the den is mine. It is small, to be sure, but provides my basic needs. It has a red sofa with fabric that is worn and frayed. If Clara had her way, it would have been banished to sofa heaven years ago. (It has too many memories for me to discard.) Up against the window overlooking Lake Superior is my oak desk. This is where I did my writing, first on a manual typewriter and then on a computer. I say that in past tense since my arthritis prevents all but the most essential writing. Now, only my dictionary and thesaurus remain on the desk. They were my workhorses, receiving extensive use as I searched for that elusive *stronger verb* or that more descriptive noun. Samuel Clemens purportedly said, "The difference between the right word and the almost right word is the difference between lightning and a lightning bug." Sam was a wise man.

The walls are covered with knotty pine, although bookshelves and pictures obscure much of it. Most of the pictures I took myself: local landscapes and spring flowers. One picture is of a much younger me accepting a Pulitzer Prize for my fifth novel. I find that a bit vain, but Clara insists it remains on the wall.

The bookshelves are where I store my memories and contain the more important books I have read over the years.

Even now, as I look at the titles and then close my eyes, I can replay the stories in vivid detail. My memory is one of the few physical attributes that has not exsanguinated with age. My other senses have been relegated to the endangered species list. Despite three laser surgeries, doctors predict diabetes will claim my eyesight within a year.

Twenty-three books on my shelf have my name on the spine. I hope that is a worthy legacy of my life. It is a silly thing for an old man to think about. I pull an old, leather-bound book from the top shelf and add it to the insulin in my plastic bag. Of all the books on the shelf, this is the book I hold in highest esteem—even above those I have authored. I close the door to the den behind me and exit the cabin through the back door.

It will be a warm day. The matutinal sun is already above the trees, suffusing the clearing in which the cabin stands with sunlight. The radiant warmth feels good on my skin. I head down a well-worn path into the woods, a trip I take daily in the summer. The path is lined on both sides by trilliums, a sure sign of spring. It is one of nature's eternal truths; trilliums will be blooming in spring thousands of years after maggots have finished dining on my soul. About one hundred yards into the woods, the path opens into a clearing of sorts. The trees still provide a canopy overhead, but the ground has been cleared of underbrush revealing a small brook. It is too small to qualify as a stream or even a creek. It is only two feet across at its widest spot and in the dry summer months is almost non-existent. The brook drains down from the hill above the cabin and culminates in a gentle waterfall of no more than three feet in height. The water gurgles as it cascades from one rock to the next.

I sit down on a reclining lawn chair I keep there for that purpose; even the short walk from the cabin leaves me tired. I write in my den, but this is where I think. The formula for a good novel, I have discovered, is two parts thinking and one part writing. I take the insulin and syringe from the bag and draw up 100 units; it fills the syringe. Then I inject it into the subcutaneous tissue of my belly. I do not bother with the perfunctory alcohol swab.

I take the book out of the bag and caress the aged leather binding. Books have been my life, my sole reason for existence. That had not always been the case. I close my eyes and remember that summer day in 1954. The war in Korean had ended and times were good. I remember standing before that square edifice of red brick and stone that squatted on a small knoll overlooking Union Street. Its windows were tall and slender and arched at the top like a cathedral. Their lower ledges were well over six feet tall, precluding any thought of peering in—not that I cared to—and the door to the building was recessed in a cave-like structure covered by a high, vaulted arch of cut stone. A drawbridge would not have been out of place. Above the arch, etched in sandstone, was *Carnegie Public Library, Sparta, Michigan*.

I had walked past the building on my way to school, but I had never been inside. I had walked past many buildings on my way to school, none as formidable as that stone fortress now peering down on me. No other building so totally dominated the landscape or so filled me with trepidation.

School was out for the summer, and fifth grade wouldn't begin until fall; I could find no logical reason for my being there. Summers were for fun and excitement. I should be standing on the pitcher's mound throwing fastballs in Little League and bowing to cheering crowds. Someday I would stand on the pitcher's mound at Tiger Stadium. When I closed my eyes I could hear the roar of the crowd as my fastball whipped over the plate for strike three. This was not to be; a cast on my right wrist prohibited any fastballs. I was out for the season.

With the summer in ruins and nothing significant to occupy my time, I had been relegated to errand boy, returning a library book for my mother. It was a degrading chore at best: books were for girls; baseball was for boys. My mother asked that I personally give the book to Mrs. Weaver, one of the librarians and a close friend of my mother's. According to my mother, Mrs. Weaver was a full-blooded Ojibwa. Weaver didn't sound very Indian to me.

Once I was assured none of my friends was watching, I slipped into the library. The inside was smaller than I had imagined. It was one large room with rows of bookshelves lined up like fields of corn. They were so tall I would have been unable to reach the top shelf, if for some unforeseen circumstance the need should arise. In the center, sitting at a large oak desk, guarding the books, was an elderly lady with hair that was not gray, but white like freshly fallen snow, and it billowed up in a bun like a snowdrift. Her skin was unusually tanned for this early in the summer. Hanging around her neck by a chain were a pair of turtle-shell glasses, a fitting accouterment to her profession. The name plaque on her desk identified her as Minne Weaver.

"Mrs. Weaver?" I said as I cautiously approached the desk as one would a trial judge.

She looked up and scrutinized all four-foot-two of me, paying particular attention to the flaming red hair protruding from under my Detroit Tigers baseball cap. "You must be Sean Connolly. I talked to your mother yesterday."

We had not previously met, but with my red hair, I was not difficult to pick out of a crowd. As the summer progressed, my face would be covered with freckles. The red hair I could tolerate; the freckles I could do without.

"Are you really an Indian?" I asked. "You don't look like an Indian." My mother would have been horrified by my question, but it was something any ten-year-old would need to know.

"You don't look much like Daniel Boone either," she replied. "You're thinking of historical Indians like you see in the movies." She opened her purse and pulled out a well-worn picture. "This is my grandfather."

I looked at the man in the black and white picture. He had dark skin and high cheekbones, and his hair was dark with braids on both sides. Although he was wearing an old-style, tailored suit, he was very much an Indian. I could visualize him riding scout for John Wayne.

"There are quite a few Indians in the Upper Peninsula where I grew up," she said. "My husband and I married after college. John worked for the mines as a geologist. When he died four years ago, I moved down here to work in the library."

Her eyes began to water—old people tend to get sentimental at times. I felt bad; I had only wanted to know if she was Indian. She grabbed a tissue from her desk and dabbed her eyes dry as if no explanation were needed.

"My mother asked me to return this book." I laid the book on her desk hoping the distraction would alleviate her sorrow.

She checked the due-date and set the book on a rolling cart half filled with books. Then she gave my red hair and cap another once over. "You must be a Tigers fan."

"Yes, ma'am. I'm going to play for the Detroit Tigers when I grow up. My uncle promised to take me to one of their games when he comes home from Korea." I looked down self-consciously at the cast on my wrist. "I fell off my friend's horse a couple of weeks ago and broke my wrist. I'd be playing ball now if it weren't for this." I held up my cast as exhibit "A."

"That can happen to any ballplayer. Even Casey had his bad days."

"Casey? Who'd he play for?" I had baseball cards for Babe Ruth, Ty Cobb, Mickey Mantle, and all the baseball greats, but I couldn't remember anyone named Casey. He had to be a minor leaguer.

"You never heard of Mighty Casey of the Mudville Nine?"

I felt a bit of shame. "No, ma'am."

"We need to correct that. I'll be right back." The lady disappeared into the cornfields and reappeared with a well-worn book. "Take this home and read "Casey at the Bat" on page twenty-nine." She handed me the book. The title of the book was *The Best of American Poetry*. I felt trapped. The noose was tightening around my neck and the trap door quivered beneath my feet. I couldn't just give the book back to her.

"Just make sure you return it in two weeks."

I left the library with the book of poetry under my shirt. If any of my friends were to see it, I'd never survive the razzing…and poetry of all books. Ten years old and my manhood was already in question. I gave the baseball field a wide berth to avoid any encounters with close friends and arrived home with my pride intact. I yelled a quick "hello" to my mother who was fixing dinner in the kitchen and headed upstairs to my room. I didn't feel safe until my bedroom door was securely closed behind me. I would hide the book under my mattress and smuggle it back into the library the following morning. No one would be the wiser.

Before Mighty Casey was sequestered in the safety of my mattress, I had to see who he was. I turned to page 29, finding "Casey At The Bat" by Ernest Lawrence Thayer.

The outlook wasn't brilliant for the Mudville nine that day.

The score stood four to two, with but one inning more to play,

And then when Cooney died at first, and Barrows did the same,

A pall-like silence fell upon the patrons of the game.

The legendary Harry Caray couldn't have better described the game. I continued reading down the page, fascinated with the rhythm of the story. It was as if I were there or at least listening to the play-by-play description on the radio. I had no doubt Mighty Casey would save the day.

Oh, somewhere in this favored land the sun is shining bright,

The band is playing somewhere, and somewhere hearts are light,

And somewhere men are laughing, and little children shout;

But there is no joy in Mudville? Mighty Casey has struck out.

The ending was a let down; I had wanted Casey to clear the bases. This was unlike any poetry I had ever read. There was no flowery language or mushy romance. It was a poem a boy could read without shame, not that I planned to tell anyone. I scanned the table of contents but found no more baseball poems. "The Midnight Ride of Paul Revere" piqued my interest; I liked horses. I turned to page 89.

Listen my children and you shall hear

Of the midnight ride of Paul Revere,

For the next few minutes I rode "through every Middlesex village and farm, for the country folk to be up and to arm." I could feel the wind in my face as my trusty steed galloped through the countryside. The horse's mane stung as it whipped across my cheek, but I didn't care. I rode through Lexington and on to Concord, all the time yelling, "The British are coming! The British are coming!" Finding nothing more of interest in the book, I stashed it under my mattress.

I returned to the library the following morning, my book safely tucked under my shirt. Mrs. Weaver was sitting at her desk overlooking her domain. I assumed defending her desk against all comers was part of her job description.

"Good morning, Mrs. Weaver. I'm returning your book."

"What did you think of 'Casey at the Bat'?"

"It was O.K., I guess. Is he a real person?"

"He can be if you want him to. Did you read any other poems?"

I wondered if conversations with librarians were privileged like talking to a priest or an attorney. "I read about Paul Revere."

"Ah, Longfellow, one of my favorite poets. Let me show you something."

She reached into one of her desk drawers and pulled out a brown paper bag. Inside was a book aged by time. It was bound in brown leather and trimmed in gold leaf. For a moment I feared she was going to pawn another book on me.

"This is one of the earliest editions of Longfellow's *Song of Hiawatha*. I'm told it's worth a lot of money—not that I would ever sell it. It tells about the adventures of a young Indian boy about your age named Hiawatha. Longfellow personally gave it to my grandfather." She opened it to the first page. "See." I looked at the page and saw Henry Wadsworth Longfellow scribbled in the margin. "My grandfather gave it to my mother, and she gave it to me. I had hoped to pass it on to my son or daughter, but John and I never had any children." Her eyes began to water again. She seemed to get teary-eyed every time she talked about her husband.

She opened the book to one of the earlier pages. "Listen to this: *By the shores of Gitche Gumee by the shining Big-Sea-Water stood the wigwam of Nokomis.*"

"What's gitche gumee?"

"That's the Indian name for Lake Superior, where I grew up. Longfellow uses a lot of Indian names." She closed the book and carefully returned it to her paper bag. "Most people call me Minne, but my real name is Minnehaha. My mother named me after Hiawatha's lover. Minnehaha means waterfall in Dakota."

"Does the book have any horses in it?"

"I don't believe so. You like horses?"

"Yes, ma'am. I have a friend who lives on a horse farm. We ride them sometimes. That's how I broke my wrist. The horse got spooked and I fell off. It wasn't his fault."

"You fell off a horse and broke your wrist and you still like horses?"

"Yes, ma'am. When you fall off a horse you got to get right back on. Mom won't let me ride until the cast comes off, but then I'm going to get right back on that horse."

"You remind me of Alec Ramsay."

"Who's he?"

"He's a boy a bit older than you but has your red hair and freckles. He has his very own horse."

"Wow, I wish I had my own horse."

"If I remember right, Alec spent the summer with his uncle who was a missionary in India. On returning home, his ship sank in a storm. Luckily for Alec, the ship had a wild horse on board. Both Alec and the horse were thrown overboard. Alec grabbed the rope tied around the horse's neck, and the horse pulled him to the safety of a small island. No one survived the shipwreck to claim the horse, so the horse became Alec's."

"Some people have all the luck. Nothing that exciting ever happens to me. Does Alec live around here?"

"Yes, I believe he does...Let me check."

Mrs. Weaver slowly walked over to one of the stacks as if each step inflicted considerable pain. I hadn't noticed that before. I assumed she had arthritis. A lot of old folks did. She returned with a book in hand, obviously for me—she had tricked me again.

"This is *The Black Stallion* by Walter Farley. I think you'll like it," she said. She gave me the book, which I was obliged to take. "Make sure you return it in two weeks."

"Yes, ma'am," I said.

I returned home with the book again hidden under my shirt and immediately took it to my room. Out of curiosity I flipped through the pages. Scattered among the sheets of prose were drawings in black ink. One showed a black horse rearing up on its hind legs. The horse had bulging muscles that rippled and gleamed like those of a prizefighter. He was sleek and mean looking, not the kind of horse that would tolerate a saddle.

I opened to the first page: *The tramp steamer Drake plowed away from the coast of India and pushed its blunt prow into the Arabian Sea...*I was on page 14 when my mother called me for dinner. The Drake was in a terrible storm and had been struck by lightning; it was beginning to sink. People were heading toward the lifeboats; the situation didn't look good.

After supper I asked to be excused so I could organize my baseball cards. It was not an unusual request; I often spent many hours with my baseball cards. I felt bad about the lie, but there was no way I could leave Alec in the middle of that storm with the ship sinking. I read well into the evening.

In the summer my parents let me stay up until ten o'clock. By then the Black Stallion had dragged Alec to a small deserted island, undoubtedly saving his life, but the Black Stallion was still a wild beast capable of killing Alec at any moment.

"Sean, time to turn off the lights."

I looked at the clock on my dresser. It was hard to believe it was already ten. I dog-eared my page and placed the book in its secure spot under my mattress. I turned off the light and lay in bed wondering how Alec would survive on the island without food and water. Finally, I could endure no more. I found a flashlight in my closet and crawled under the covers so my parents wouldn't see my light shining on the ground from their bedroom window, and I read late into the night. When I awoke in the morning the batteries to my flashlight were dead. The book lay on the floor with a dog-ear marking the place I had stopped. I finished the book in two days.

I found Mrs. Weaver sitting at her desk as usual, the desk piled high with stacks of books. I placed *The Black Stallion* on a vacant spot on her desk. "I enjoyed the book," I said.

She looked up at me and smiled as if she knew I would. "He's quite the horse, isn't he?"

"Even with his cut foot, he beat both Sun Raider and Cyclone. The race wasn't even close."

"He also won the Kentucky Derby," Mrs. Weaver added.

"No, ma'am," I said. "The race was in Chicago." I hated to correct her, but she was clearly mistaken.

"That was the race against Sun Raider and Cyclone. You don't think the Black Stallion stopped racing after Chicago, do you?"

She must have seen the confusion on my face. "Follow me," she said. She picked up *The Black Stallion* and headed toward the cornfield, walking slowly, obviously in pain. She stopped at an aisle labeled *juvenile* and headed down the row, stopping midway down the aisle. "These are the F's," she said. "The books are in alphabetical order by the author's last name. All these books were written by Walter Farley." She returned *The Black Stallion* to the stack.

I looked at the books in amazement. There were *The Black Stallion Returns, Son of the Black Stallion, The Black Stallion Revolts, The Black Stallion Mystery*. There must have been fifteen or more books in all.

"Walter Farley wrote a whole series about the Black Stallion." She pulled out *The Black Stallion Returns*. "This is the second book in the series."

"Can I read that one?" I asked.

She gave me the book. "Bring it back in two weeks."

I left the library with my treasure firmly gripped in my hands. I didn't care who saw me. I would read every one of the Black Stallion books; I had all summer. I finished reading *The Black Stallion Returns* in three days and returned for another book. Each time I read a book, Mrs. Weaver would quiz me about the story. I didn't need much encouragement; I was always willing to tell her about Alec's adventures.

Summer passed by too quickly. By late August I had read eight of the books. With two weeks left before school started, it seemed unlikely I would complete the series. Homework would make finding time for reading difficult. With *The Black Stallion*

Revolts under my arm, I walked into the library. It was unusually quiet even for a library. I walked over to the main desk. Instead of Mrs. Weaver, a man in his late forties was sitting at her desk. I felt a bit of anger; he had no right to be there. That was Mrs. Weaver's desk.

"Where's Mrs. Weaver?" I demanded as if the man had personally hidden her away somewhere.

The man looked up at me paying particular attention to the red hair under my Detroit Tigers' baseball cap. "Mrs. Weaver died last night," he said, choosing his words carefully. "She had cancer, you know. She had been in a lot of pain."

I was overcome with shock. What the man was telling me couldn't be true. I wanted to run out of the library and never come back, but my feet wouldn't respond. I just stared at the man in disbelief.

"You must be Sean Connolly."

"Yes, sir."

"Mrs. Weaver spoke very highly of you." He reached into Mrs. Weaver's desk drawer and pulled out a package. It was wrapped in plain brown paper and had a card taped to the outside. "She wanted you to have this."

I thanked the man and quickly left the library; I didn't want anyone to see me cry, but I cried all the way home. I went straight to my room so my mother wouldn't see the tears in my eyes. I set the package on my bed, preferring not to open it as if opening the package would somehow confirm Mrs. Weaver's death. Then, I cried quietly for another ten minutes. She had given me a new life filled with fun and adventure, and now she had taken it away. It wasn't right.

The card attached to the package said simply, "Sean Connolly." I removed the card from the package—my mother always insisted I read the card first. I recognized Mrs. Weaver's meticulous handwriting. She wrote with a flourish that made me envious. My teachers always told me my handwriting left something to be desired.

"When you read this you will know that I am gone," she wrote. "Summer went by too quickly, but you made my last days enjoyable. Please don't cry for me. I am happy now, for I am Minnehaha the waterfall, and I must return to my homeland. I have gone to join my Hiawatha, and together we shall walk along *the shores of Gitche Gumee by the shining Big-Sea-Water*. If you come to visit, which I hope you do, you will find me in the mournful cry of the loon or the chirp of the cricket or the susurration of the gentle waterfall. I will be there for you."

I set the card aside, my eyes still filled with tears. I would never read another book without thinking of her. I knew what it was before I opened the package and pulled out the book. It was bound in aged brown leather and decorated with gold leaf. On the cover, printed in gold leaf, was—*The Song of Hiawatha*.

I caress the old leather binding with tired, arthritic fingers as I have done so many times in the past. Even with my eyes closed, I can identify every crease, every imperfection, as if such a book could have imperfections. The book has lost none of its magic over the years. Just holding it gives me an ineffable pleasure that even I cannot express in words.

Around me crickets are chirping, and down by the lake, a loon is voicing its lonely, mournful cry. The day is becoming cool. I feel a chill cut through my body, although a sheen of sweat covers my skin. I try to lift my hand to my throbbing head, but lack the strength. Vaguely I feel each heartbeat pounding within my chest, as adrenaline tries to compensate for the lack of glucose flowing in my blood. My heart races. It is a race it cannot win. My thoughts begin to fog. Where am I? I wonder. The crickets have ceased their chirping, as if to observe a moment of silence, and I can no longer hear the loon down by the lake. All I hear is the susurration of a gentle waterfall—and then there is silence.

14

Junior and Senior High School

Junior high offered a new experience. We no longer had one dedicated teacher but rotated from classroom to classroom and were taught by teachers who specialized in math, science, or English. I also noticed that half of my classmates were strangers. They were not the kids who shared my classroom since kindergarten. I had heard rumors of one-room classrooms in the farmlands, but I never gave it much thought. They had such interesting names such as: White, Koon, Englishville, Buck, Boyd, Colton, Piersol, Manchester, and Meyers. Now I was confronted by the sons and daughters of farmers who were educated in those schools.

Koon School — Sparta Historical Commission Photo

Everyone had a homeroom where they reported for their first class. Fran Ebers (now Rollert) sat behind me in our 7th grade study hall. She received her first seven years of education at Koon School. She describes her school as having one large classroom at the top of a flight of stairs. A heavy cord at the landing on the top of the stairs led to a bell that Mrs. Thome used to call the students in from recess. There were also bookshelves filled with books that never changed. A cloak room off from the classroom provided a place to hang coats, and a bathroom was located at the end of the cloak room. With students spread over seven grades it was difficult for Mrs. Thome to provide much individual attention. Fran says she felt like she was on her own most of the time and did not get the same quality education as the city kids. She graduated from Western Michigan University and went on to get a Masters Degree from the University of Missouri, so she did not do so badly.

Interior of Buck School   Courtsey of John Anderson

John Anderson went to Buck School, which was a wooden one-room school house. John says a bookmobile appeared every month and students could pick one book. None of the students was bussed. John walked 1.4 miles one way to get to school, which is a long distance for short legs. If you ask John, I am sure he will confirm it was up-hill in both directions. John and I were both nerds, so we struck up a friendship that lasted well past high school. John thought his education at Buck School was just as good as the education received in town. Since the students in the one-room schools had the same teacher for seven years, the quality of education probably varied depending on the teacher. I thought the farm kids were just as well educated as I was. I think they had one advantage over the city kids; they knew how to study on their own. This became a valuable skill as we progressed in our education.

Schools were not the fortresses they are today. The doors were not locked, and anyone could walk in from the street. We had no security guards. We did live in a gun society. My father was an avid pheasant hunter as were many older boys and men in Sparta. My older brother and I had BB guns from an early age. We used them for target practice and to hunt frogs along Nash Creek. Once my older brother hunted our grandparents' chickens. Jack was a good shot, but received no applause. I believe he paid for the dead chicken out of his allowance.

At age twelve I was eligible to obtain a small game license and hunt pheasants with my father. My father would not even consider it until I took a hunter safety course. It was sponsored by the NRA and taught by Bill Pearl who was also a city cop. The NRA had a better reputation in those days. It was an organization of hunters concerned with gun safety. Jack and I enjoyed the course. We even got to target practice with .22 caliber rifles in the basement of the Catholic Church. There were no chickens for Jack to shoot, but we did have bull's eye targets. A piece of sheet metal slanted at a 45 degree angle bounced the bullets into a box of sand.

Many other teenagers hunted pheasants, and it was not uncommon for a high school student to drive to school with a shotgun in the car. Some pickup trucks even had a gun rack over the back window. No one was concerned. In the '50s and '60s it was inconceivable that someone would buy an assault weapon designed to hunt people.

Guns were still dangerous. This became painfully apparent one summer after my sophomore year in high school. A class mate of mine named Tim Korreck was hunting crows with a .22 caliber rifle. He was hunting alone and accidentally shot himself. According to the official report, he crawled twenty feet before he died. He was a classmate, and we were devastated. People our age were not supposed to die. We didn't blame the gun. We assumed Tim violated one of the safety rules. If this happened today, the school would bring in counselors to help students cope with the emotional grief. Time heals all wounds and we eventually overcame our grief.

The endless cheeseburgers ceased when my father sold the B & T. Even with my longer legs there was insufficient time to walk home for lunch. Fortunately, my grandparents lived ten minutes from school, and my grandmother was a fantastic cook. Two years later I graduated to the high school where they had a cafeteria.

High school offered the opportunity to pick our own subjects. Under pressure from my parents, I signed up for four years of English, but my heart wasn't in it. My grades reflected my heart. I could not spell, and any paper I wrote was severely marked down because of spelling errors. English teachers suggested I look up words I did not know how to spell. For a 500 word essay that would require looking up 500 words. Have you ever noticed that even dictionaries expect you to know the correct spelling? By the time I arrived in high school, computers had made their appearance, but a computer with the power of a modern laptop filled a large room. They were not available to the general public. Spell check was still a pipe dream.

All our work was submitted in longhand or via a typewriter. If a student made an error on a typewriter, the student painted over the error with fast-drying white paint from a bottle similar to fingernail polish. A large mistake required ripping the sheet of paper out of the typewriter and starting over. That is why I gravitated to math and science.

Typing was considered a secretarial subject and therefore a "girl's" course. My father had three years of college but could not type. He was fast with two fingers. He knew this would not be adequate for the future. He ensured that all his sons took typing. His wisdom proved prophetic.

Our superintendent was a man named Bill DeHart. He was a fixture at the school and must have been superintendent for decades. I cannot remember a time when he was not superintendent. He was a fascinating individual to listen to. One of his favorite sayings was, "It is no longer smart to be dumb." All too often people looked down on nerds and students with good grades. He was quick to point out that these were the individuals who would rule our future.

Mr. DeHart loved to substitute when a teacher suddenly fell ill or was otherwise incapacitated, and we all enjoyed having him. He had a wealth of knowledge on any topic. I was in advanced biology class in my sophomore year when Mr. Wever was absent for some unknown reason. We were all pleased when Mr. DeHart arrived. I don't remember what brought up the topic, but he asked if anyone knew where Laos was. No one raised a hand. I had never heard of the country and would have guessed somewhere in Africa or South America. Then he asked if we had heard of Vietnam. Again no one raised a hand. I wondered why such obscure countries were worthy of our conversation. He advised us to watch those countries because they would become politically important in the near future. He described countries filled with jungles and unstable governments. I could see little value in either country. That opinion would change drastically in the coming years.

A heavy drizzle watered the dried-out grass on November 22, 1963. The sky was uniformly gray, and it appeared the rain would continue throughout the day. At 1:30 in the afternoon, I was in English class. Mr. Dehart was in a meeting with school board members, when his secretary passed him a note; President Kennedy had been shot in Dallas! The first we heard about it was when Mr. DeHart's voice came over the intercom connected to all the classrooms. He offered little information other than that the President had been shot. At that time, no one knew how serious the President's wounds were. Mr. DeHart said he would play the radio or TV audio over the intercom. If any teacher did not wish to listen, they were to send a note to the office asking to have the sound turned off in their room. No teacher sent a note to the office. We all listened to the broadcast. It was obvious the newscasters did not know the extent of the injuries. We listened in silence.

The bell rang and we filed out and headed toward the next classroom. Normally, there is chatter and laughter as students walked to the next classroom. There was only silence. Several girls had tears in their eyes. My next class was on the west side of the building. Sometime after 2 pm the radio announcer on the intercom informed us that President John F. Kennedy was dead. The classroom continued in silence as we listened to the details. This was beyond our comprehension. This should not happen in America.

The windows of the classroom provided a good view of the lawn in front of the school. Centered on the lawn was a large flag pole. The flag was never flown in bad weather. With all the rain, this day was not an exception. I gave the flagpole little thought until I saw our custodian, Al Dykstra, walking into the rain with an American flag under his arm. Mr. Dykstra was a Dutch immigrant with a very heavy accent. He was always popular with the students. A normal person would have run out to the flag

Al Dykstra

pole to minimize exposure to the constant drizzle, but not Mr. Dykstra. He solemnly walked up to the pole and attached the flag to the rope. He raised the flag to the top of the pole and then lowered it to half-staff. I was unaware at the time that that was the proper way of placing the flag at half-staff. Perhaps it was only rain drops, but I thought I saw tears on his cheeks. He may have been born in the Netherlands, but he was an American.

We graduated in June of 1964. I had known many of my classmates since kindergarten. Some of the rural students I met in seventh grade were now close friends. I think we were all a bit tearful at graduation knowing we might never see some of our friends again. Many of us were heading to college, others were moving away from Sparta in search of employment. For us boys/men the military draft and Vietnam hung heavily on our shoulders. Mr. DeHart's prediction was coming true.

15

Grand Rapids Junior College

It was an assumption in our household that everyone would go to college. I had no alternate plans, and my friends were heading to college. It made sense. College also provided a temporary draft deferment. I enrolled at Grand Rapids Junior College (now G.R. Community College), but I lacked motivation or purpose. I still preferred science. I had an unquenchable curiosity and needed to understand how things worked. Fortunately, my parents were forgiving when my pet cecropia moth laid eggs on my bedroom wall. My mother was less forgiving when the eggs hatched the following spring. I had caterpillars crawling all over my room.

Then there were the rocket years. NASA was putting satellites into space with rockets, and I thought I also needed a rocket. In my defense, I must point out that NASA had rockets that exploded on the launch paid. My rocket didn't explode, but it did launch prematurely in my bedroom. It whirled around the room before it finally landed on my wooden desk. I tried to explain to my parents that it was mostly smoke, but the burned curtains said otherwise, and I had a large hole in my desk. That ended my career in rocketry, but I still loved chemistry and science. I chose chemistry for my major. To save money I formed a car pool with Dave Piell, Larry Fonger, Sandy Stevens and Jack Sands.

Larry Fonger was my undoing. We both liked chess and found that more entertaining than homework. We played for money. It was always double or nothing. I was a better chess player than Larry, and I think at one time he owed me several million dollars. To be honest, I didn't always play fair. I had a chess set that had inadvertently included three black bishops. Somewhere within the mid-game I would sneak the third bishop onto the playing board. Sometimes Larry would not discover the deception until the endgame when his King was confronted by three black bishops. Larry would get mad more at himself than me and declare the game void. I enjoyed those "voids" more than I did winning. I did it time after time, and he seldom caught me until the end.

There are consequences to not doing homework. I received a D in the first semester of calculus. I continued on to the second semester and also received a D. I repeated this class and got a C on the second time around. That was an improvement. I flunked analytical chemistry, which was supposed to be my major. Matriculating at a college is not sufficient for a draft deferment—the draft board expected progress. Consequently, I made many trips to the draft board to plead my case. I became good friends with a lady named Dorothy who was in charge of my fate. I made it through the first year of college, but it was not impressive.

Our car pool fell apart in the second year. I believe Larry Fonger dropped out of school, and Sandy Stevens transferred to a nursing dormitory at Butterworth Hospital. Jack Sands and I signed up to stay at the YMCA, which was a block away from J.C. The YMCA had five or six floors. Each room had a bed and a desk and a window, but nothing more. The bathroom was down the hall. Lodging was about $11 or $12 per week. This was cheaper than driving from Sparta each day. The second semester I became a floor resident assistant, and my room became free.

I blame Jack Sands for my downfall in the second year of college (It was never my fault). There was a small pocket park in front of the YMCA. It was our playground in the late evening. Jack and I along with several other YMCA residents would hang out in the park and shoot the breeze. The YMCA was very conservative, so there was never any alcohol or drugs. We were crazy enough without medicinal help. In the center of the park were a small fountain and a pool of water. I doubt if the water was twelve inches deep. We often rolled up our pant legs and waded in the pool. Once on a dare I was talked into making a swan dive into the pool. I knew the pool was shallow, but I assumed if I belly flopped all would turn out well. I gave my wallet to Jack, so it would not get wet and then made the most beautiful belly flop—clothes and all. The water was shallower than I thought. My nose and forehead scraped against the concrete bottom. I was lucky I didn't break my nose. The abrasions took over a week to heal.

To help pay for my tuition and my room at the YMCA I got a job at the college cleaning lounges. I hated that job. The worst part was cleaning the ash trays. Nothing is worse than the smell of old cigarette butts. After two weeks on the job, a classmate told me the Grand Rapids Press was hiring college students to answer phones. Anything had to be better than cleaning ashtrays. I applied for the job and began working a week later. It was in the circulation department. People would call to cancel or start a subscription. There were four of us students answering the phones and writing down orders. I worked four hours on week-day evenings and eight hours on Saturday. I wasn't rich, but I could pay for my room and tuition. There was even enough remaining money to purchase one double-meat hamburger and fries at a local greasy spoon. When I went home on weekends, my mother fattened me up. She thought one hamburger a day was insufficient nourishment.

One of the perks of working for the Grand Rapids Press was free newspapers. They always had a stack of free papers near the door for employees. I had several nursing student friends at Butterworth Hospital, which was not far from the college. After work I would take a copy to their dorm. Not only did my nursing student friends enjoy it, but it also put me in the good graces of the nursing dorm receptionist who guarded the premises with a vigilant eye. She always read the paper before it got passed on to my friends.

I didn't have any long-term girlfriends in college. With Vietnam hovering over me, I did not want to place others at emotional risk. It was not that I was ignoring girls, it was quite the opposite. One night I took a nursing student to a movie and returned her to her dorm by 11 p.m. Then Jack Sands and I picked up his girlfriend and her friend for a double date of bowling. They both got out of work at midnight.

My grades didn't do any better in the second year. I enjoyed learning and had an insatiable curiosity. I just didn't want to learn at the pace that college demanded. One of the employees at the *Grand Rapids Press* was a WW II veteran. We were once talking about war in general. He was in college when he was drafted. He said after the war he had no desire to go back to college. His words haunted me for the next several years. I feared after two years in the military I would no longer have a desire to learn or return to school. I vowed I would not let that happen.

During the winter of my second year my grandfather asked if I would be willing to accompany him to Honduras in Central American. My aunt and uncle were missionaries in Tegucigalpa, and he wanted to visit them. He offered to pay my way. My grandmother had recently died, and he didn't want to go alone. If I accepted the invitation, I would miss two weeks of classes. I did not think twice. It was a wonderful experience that I will never forget. I have never regretted my decision, but I added organic chemistry and second term German to my list of failed classes. After two years of college I had a GPA of 1.67. Dorothy at the draft board declared that insufficient progress. I did not like her decision, but I couldn't disagree with her assessment. The paperwork was set in motion. I would be formally drafted in the fall.

Then something happened that changed the rest of my life. I don't know where I saw it. It may have been in the *Grand Rapids Press* or it could have been posted on the help wanted board at the college. Action Ambulance needed ambulance attendants. This was a professional ambulance company in Grand Rapids. What teen-ager would not want to ride in an ambulance with lights flashing and sirens blaring? I applied for the job and to my surprise was hired.

In the sixties there was little regulation of ambulances. In many small communities the ambulance service was run by the local funeral home. This made sense. Morticians knew their anatomy and physiology, and they were on-call 24-7. The state did have some regulations; I had to pass a standard and advanced first aid course. This was taught at the ambulance barn during a Saturday afternoon. At the end of the day, I was a qualified ambulance attendant. I got to wear a fancy jacket with ambulance printed on the back. I was in hog-heaven. I couldn't drive the ambulance, because that required a chauffeur's license and you had to be twenty-one. The man who would be driving was in his forties and had worked on ambulances for over twenty years. He was also the first-aid instructor.

The ambulance was not the cracker box of today. It could be better described as a station wagon on steroids. The ambulance had room for one patient on a stretcher and had a small seat for the attendant near the patient's head. Other than placing pressure dressings on bleeding wounds or giving oxygen, there was little the attendant could do once the patient was loaded into the ambulance. The ambulance did have flashing lights and a loud siren, and I had an impressive jacket. What more could a teenager want?

Standard and advanced first aid is not a lot of training and I had no experience. I was worried that my skills might be sub-par. Fortunately, the management felt likewise. They scheduled a third person for my first day. I only had to watch. That was the game plan, except the third person called in sick. We had to make do.

Our first call was a multi-car accident at the corner of Four-Mile Road and Alpine, a very busy intersection. We were the first ambulance on the scene. I counted at least three banged up cars, and I could see several mangled bodies scattered across the street. Few cars had safety belts in the 60s, and it was not uncommon to find passengers lying on the street. I looked at the shattered bodies and froze like a rabbit. I could think of nothing I could do. Then my experienced partner calmly told me to put a pressure dressing on a bleeding wound and splint that obvious fracture. I could follow his directions, but I was incapable of independent thought.

We took one of the more severely injured patients. It was a young girl with a scalping head injury. I could see a large section of her skull. I immobilized her head with my hands while she moaned in pain. There were no cervical collars or commercial neck stabilizers. I was the neck immobilizer. Even with the lights flashing and siren blaring it took forever to reach the hospital. Fortunately, hospital personnel took over as soon as we arrived.

While my partner replaced the sheets, I walked over to a quiet section of the ER and leaned my hand against the wall. I was feeling nauseated, and it was just a matter of time before I vomited. I looked for a nearby bathroom and found none. The vomit came up my esophagus, but I swallowed it down twice. I assumed if I vomited my medical career would be over. It took me five minutes of deep breathing before I got my stomach under control. If my partner noticed, he said nothing. On the way back to the ambulance barn, he explained everything we did and why.

The following week was not as traumatic. After each run I would pepper my partner with questions. If I had placed as much effort into my college studies I would have graduated with honors. I was learning a useful trade.

We were paid a small hourly wage but received our big money when we made a run. That was the only time our employer earned money. We often listened on the police scanner. There were two ambulance companies in Grand Rapids. Central dispatch tried to alternate the ambulance calls, but if we heard of an accident on the scanner and beat the competition to the scene, the money was ours. Sometimes if we arrived just after the competitor arrived we would pull up behind the competitor's ambulance, so the back door could not be opened. Then we would grab the patient. This may seem unethical, but the competition did the same. Welcome to for-profit medical care.

By the end of the summer I had become quite proficient. My partner was a great teacher. I only wish I could remember his name. I also discovered I enjoyed treating injured people. But summer was over, and I had to prepare for two years of military service and most likely a year in Vietnam.

16

U.S. Army Induction

I thought they would just ship me off to some army base, but getting drafted is complicated. I received orders in the mail to report to the Greyhound bus station in Grand Rapids for a trip to Fort Wayne. I immediately thought of Fort Wayne, Indiana, but further inspection of the document revealed it was a small military installation near Detroit. We rated a chartered bus. A man possibly from the draft board checked off our names as we loaded onto the bus. Rumor on the bus suggested we were scheduled for a physical exam and academic evaluations. Perhaps if I were lucky the physicians would find diabetes or some other non-fatal illness that would cause rejection. Unfortunately, I felt healthy. There were many theories on how best to flunk the physical exam. One individual suggested ingesting a small piece of aluminum foil would mimic a stomach ulcer on X-rays. Other individuals had packets of sugar that they intended to add to their urine. I sat in silence.

As far as a military base, Fort Wayne was a disappointment. I saw little more than a cluster of old buildings, and there were few people in uniform. We were ushered into a large room with multiple tables. Someone who appeared to be in charge called out our names. After our drivers' licenses confirmed our identities, we were told to strip and place our belongings in a sealed bag. It was obvious the military was not concerned with modesty. I wondered where individuals were hiding their sugar packets. Henry Ford would have been impressed with the assembly line physical. One physician walked down the line listening to heart and lungs while someone else checked eyes, ears, and nose. We were then asked to squat and move our arms windmill fashion. We were directed to pee in a cup under a watchful eye. I could not have added sugar to the urine even if I had a sugar packet. They drew blood at the last station. In the military you do not give blood; they take it.

In the afternoon we were given a packet of forms to complete. I assumed one was an I.Q. test. Other documents requested educational and work experience. There was no box for college flunky, so I put down two years of college. It may have been bragging, but I did have enough credits to qualify for junior status. For work experience I added ambulance attendant and phone monitoring specialist for my work at the *Grand Rapids Press*. I didn't think sanitation engineer for cleaning ash trays was relevant.

We must have passed the physical, because an officer in class A uniform arrived to tell us what a great honor it was to serve our country. There were about forty of us. I was in the back. The officer asked us to raise our right hands. I think I was the only one not raising the right hand. The officer read the induction oath and everyone said I do—except for me. It was my moment of defiance. I was still a civilian. Unfortunately, I was the only individual aware of that status. We returned to Grand Rapids on our charter bus.

I received another letter in the mail a few days later directing me to report to the Grand Rapids train station. This time they were serious; the listed destination was Fort Knox. I assumed I was not going to protect the gold bullion. I had never been on a train before, so the first hour was interesting. The novelty quickly wore off. It was a long trip to Fort Knox.

The train did not go directly to Fort Knox. We debarked from the train and men in uniform politely loaded us into busses. I didn't discover until later that they were only polite because we were in a civilian area. That changed when the bus arrived at

Fort Knox. The yelling began as soon as we stepped down from the bus. It only added confusion to an already confusing situation. It was late in the day. We were fed and assigned a barracks. The barracks consisted of one large room with two rows of bunk beds with an aisle down the middle. The latrine was at the far end of the barracks. The latrine had a row of sinks and a row of toilets. Privacy was not an option.

The following morning began before dawn; Sgt. Barns arrived with whistle in hand to rouse the troops. He gave us fifteen minutes to use the latrine, get dressed, and form up in front of the barracks. Sgt. Barn's concept of "form up" was vastly different than ours. We stood around in a large cluster of individuals. Sgt. Barns wanted us in four rows of non-individuals. It took the better part of fifteen minutes to evenly space ourselves to meet his expectation. He tried to teach us basic commands such as attention, right-face, left-face, and forward march. I think a junk-yard dog could have learned the commands faster than we did.

The drill sergeant then marched us to the mess hall. Breakfast was always the same. Cereal and milk were available. Hot entrees included scrambled eggs that were, according to rumor, made from powdered eggs. Another staple was S.O.S., which was sausage gravy on toast. The polite version was that S.O.S. stood for Same Old Stuff. There was also a more vulgar version that will not be repeated here.

After breakfast we were marched to a warehouse where we were issued military uniforms and equipment. We were beginning to look like soldiers, but not quite. Some of us had long hair. I didn't think my hair was long, but the barber did. When we left the company barbershop we all had shiny domes. Our transition from civilian life was complete. Other than height, weight, and facial features we were all the same. We were no longer individuals.

We had our pre-induction physical that said we were in good health. The military wanted to ensure we stayed that way. One morning after breakfast they marched us to the dispensary and told us to take off our shirts. As we marched by single file, medics injected us with a variety of vaccines including typhoid, plague, and other diseases I did not know still existed. They didn't use needles as one would expect. Instead, they wiped our shoulders with alcohol and then pressed a vaccination gun against our skin. High pressure forced the vaccine through the skin and into the shoulder muscle. Several men flinched and the high pressure vaccine ripped through the skin. We left the facility with painful shoulders. This was repeated six weeks later for booster shots. The plague booster shot was particularly painful. Several men had severe reactions and passed out. Fortunately, vaccination guns are no longer used.

Basic training consisted of eight weeks of marching, running, shooting, and classes on military customs. All orders and instructions were given at ten decibels above ear piercing. It created an atmosphere where people followed orders without thought.

We were issued M-14 rifles that we learned to dis-assemble in the dark. I thought that strange since the M-16 was now the standard weapon in Vietnam where I assumed we were going. I found target practice at the rifle range enjoyable. Our drill sergeants were all business and yelling was minimal. With forty people of questionable mentality, loaded weapons were always a concern.

The grenade range was even more fun. We practiced throwing dummy grenades for several days. The grenades were not thrown like a baseball using the elbow. Instead the elbow remains extended and the grenade is lobbed over the head using only the shoulder muscles. I have thrown more than one cherry bomb or M-80, but throwing a live grenade was big time. Unfortunately we only had one try.

The grenade range consisted of a long, waist-high concrete wall with a grenade-proof window that allowed us to watch the grenade explode. A three-foot deep concrete trench just in front of the wall offered a safe disposal for any grenades dropped by a scared trainee. The sergeant in charge of the grenade range was expected to kick the fallen grenade into the trench and then throw the scared private to the ground. I was disappointed that no one dropped a grenade.

Boot camp was both physically and mentally taxing. We had ten-hour days followed by an hour spent polishing boots and brass. After a week or two I started feeling depressed. In the evening I would go outside to look up at the stars. I was raised as a free-range child. Now I felt like a prisoner. There was no fence or barbed wire, but escape was not a possibility. Some individuals did go AWOL. They usually returned home where the military police were waiting for them. I had no choice but to take one day at a time.

I assumed I would be heading for infantry training after basic. That was where the army needed the most troops. That added to my depression. About three weeks before basic graduation, a recruiter arrived to offer incentives to those individuals willing to extend their enlistments by an additional year. For one additional year we could choose our advanced training or area of deployment. For one extra year I could become a medic. I must admit, it was a tempting offer. I would still be on the front lines, although I would be a medic instead of an infantryman. I really wanted to return to school. An additional year in the army did not fit into that plan. I turned down the offer.

Eight weeks is a long time, but basic training eventually came to an end. On the final day the drill sergeants ignored us—they had fresh troops arriving by bus to harass. We waited in a large room while clerks typed up our orders. We would be heading to AIT (advanced individual training) where we would learn a military skill. I knew anyone staying at Fort Knox would train in armor. That was the extent of my knowledge. The clerks passed out our travel orders and documents. I was going to Fort

Sam Houston, but there was no indication of what I would do there. Since the drill sergeants were no longer belligerent and actually friendly, I asked what kind of training they provided at Fort Sam Houston. He looked at my orders and said, "That's a medical post. You're going to be a medic." He spoke like it was a death sentence.   Combat medic was one of the more dangerous jobs in the military, but that one sentence cured my depression.

The difference between basic and AIT was like night and day. On weekends we were free to go to San Antonio, see the Alamo, and stroll along the River Walk. Unless someone screwed up, everyone was treated with respect. In basic training, we had individuals with a variety of education. We had some people who could not read or write. In AIT most of the individuals had some college background, a few had college degrees. We spent most of the day in classrooms learning anatomy, physiology, and pharmacology. It was not much different from college, except I now did the homework.

It was not all classwork. Some days we practiced splinting fractures and dressing wounds in an open field. We learned how to drag wounded soldiers to safety using pistol belts and cravats. San Antonio had good weather for such activities. On rainy days we stayed inside and practiced starting IVs and giving shots. We learned to give shots using each other's arms.

Medical technology was not as advanced in the '60s. We didn't have over-the-needle flexible sheaths for starting IVs. We used rigid metal needles and hoped the patient did not move much. Syringes were made of reusable glass. The needles were also reusable. We learned how to sharpen the needles and then wiped them with cotton to detect any burrs at the needle tip. All of the equipment needed to be meticulously packed and autoclaved.

We lived in the same barracks and attended the same classes. Over the ten weeks I made many friends. Some of these friends were conscientious objectors (COs). They were willing to participate in the military as medics, but they would not carry a gun. Five or six of them were Mormons, which was my first exposure to this religion. John Adams was about 6'2" and weighed well over 200 pounds. He presented a formidable appearance, but he was gentle as a lamb. He was also the unspoken leader of the Mormons. During the first week of our training one of the sergeants said he was going to tell an off-color joke. If anyone found such jokes offensive, they could step outside. The instructor assumed this was a rhetorical suggestion. John stood up and walked out of the room. The other Mormons followed him out. A week later the instructor wanted to tell another off-color joke. It was met with the same results. That was the last of the off-color jokes.

Another friend of mine was Allen Jagielo from San Gabriel, California. He loved to sing and had a golden voice. We had group showers, which were nothing more than a small room with numerous shower heads on the wall. Allen loved to serenade us in the shower. One evening someone suggested that his vocal talent would be wasted, since he was going to Vietnam and would get killed. We all laughed. It was a bit of gallows humor. In reality we assumed Vietnam was in all our futures. At the end of AIT, I received orders for Fort Benning, Georgia. Allen received orders for the 1st Infantry Division in Vietnam. I heard later that he died from shrapnel wounds after less than a month in Vietnam. I have seen his name on the Vietnam Memorial several times. Over 2,000 of the names on the wall belong to Army Medics and Navy Corpsmen. That is more than three and a half percent. It was not a good occupation.

Fort Benning was an infantry training site. They also trained paratroopers. I was assigned to work at a clinic for the trainees. A physician conducted sick call in the morning. We took temperatures and blood pressures before they were seen by the doctor. In the afternoon the clinic was staffed by three medics. It was boring work with plenty of free time.

I stayed in a barracks with many other medics, some of whom were in AIT with me. Mike Youngdahl was one of them.

We had become friends in AIT and the friendship continued at Fort Benning. I bought a used Nash Rambler for $250. It was my first car and provided the wheels, so Mike and I could explore Georgia.

I had a year and a half of military time left. The army did not draft me to explore the Georgia countryside. I knew Vietnam was still in my future. When I did get there, I would be on my own. I wouldn't have the experienced partner I had when working for Action Ambulance. I worried that my skills would be inadequate.

Martin Army Hospital is a full service hospital that provided healthcare service to the Fort Benning soldiers and their dependents. They had a state of the art emergency room. I decided that was the place to fine-tune my medical skills. I found a sergeant in the ER who looked like he knew what he was doing and asked if I could volunteer in the ER. He thought it was an excellent idea, but no one had ever asked to volunteer before, and he did not have the authority to grant permission. He referred me to a lieutenant. The lieutenant thought it was an excellent idea, but no one had ever asked to volunteer before, and he did not have the authority to give me permission. He referred me to a captain. Two days later I was standing outside the office of a bird colonel in charge of the hospital. She thought it was a good idea, but no one had ever asked to do extra duty in the past. Fortunately, as head of the hospital personnel she did not need anyone's permission. She told me she would make some phone calls, and I was to report to the ER the following evening.

They were expecting me when I arrived at the ER. I don't know what the colonel said, but everyone did their best to teach me ER skills. I learned to suture and assisted in motor vehicle accidents. If a physician had an interesting patient, he patiently explained the illness and the proposed treatment. What I was learning would prove immensely valuable in the coming months. With one year remaining in my enlistment, I received orders for Vietnam.

The army gave me one month's leave, since there would be no time off once I arrived in Vietnam. I drove home from Georgia and sold my Nash Rambler to my parents for one dollar. I would no longer need it. It may seem strange, but I paid a final visit to the local draft board. Dorothy was still there. She was a nice lady and I held no grudges. This visit was not about me.

I explained that I was on my way to Vietnam, and I was fulfilling my two-year obligation. I also explained that I had a brother who was giving two years of his time as a Peace Corps volunteer in Panama. His sacrifice to the nation was just as valuable as mine. She seemed to agree. Many conscientious objectors provided two years of similar service. I don't think Jack heard anymore from the draft board.

−17−
Vietnam

I arrived at Cam Ranh Bay in September of 1967. I expected to be greeted by gunfire and incoming North Vietnamese rockets. One's imagination has a way of magnifying potential hazards. Instead I was assaulted by the intense heat of the south Asian sun as I disembarked from the climate controlled cabin of a chartered commercial jetliner.

Cam Ranh Bay was one of the best deep water ports in Southeast Asia. It also had a peninsula extending far out from the mainland. The peninsula was large enough for an airport and support facilities, but it was too far from the mainland to worry about rocket or mortar attacks. I discovered no one was armed. Except for the intense heat, I could have been in a military base back home.

We were marched to a wood framed processing building where clerks typed away at computers to complete our orders. Then they issued new fatigues with cargo pockets. It was my first experience with cargo pants, and I was impressed with the storage capacity. Our jungle boots had canvas sides to dissipate sweat and two small drains on the side to drain larger quantities of water. I was hoping I would not need that feature. Wading through swamps did not sound exciting. I was told there was a metal plate in the sole of the boot to protect against sharp punji sticks. Punji sticks were made from sharpened bamboo that was often dipped in feces. Anyone stepping on a punji stick could be incapacitated for weeks.

I was soon fully outfitted and sent to a waiting cargo plane. The orders in my hand said I was heading to Camp Enari just outside of Pleiku, which the co-pilot informed me was the home base for the 4th Inf. Division. That eliminated plush jobs at a hospital. The cargo plane had few of the amenities I had experienced on the chartered commercial plane. There were several passengers, and we sat on webbed retractable seats along the wall of the plane. The center of the cabin was filled with a variety of boxes. The pilot and co-pilot had side arms, but the rest of us were unarmed. This was not what I had expected. For the most part, we flew too high for small arms fire, and as far as I knew the enemy had no anti-aircraft capability. With no windows, it was a boring flight.

After two hours the cargo plane glided to a perfect landing at a small airstrip on the outskirts of Pleiku. It was not much of an airport with only a few fixed-winged aircraft, but there were row after row of Huey helicopters. I had seen them on the evening news, but this was the first time I had seen them up close and personal. I gave my orders to a clerk who greeted us upon landing. He directed me to one of the Hueys that was taking supplies to Camp Enari. I was told it was a short ride— only 12 kilometers southeast of Pleiku. I had to admit; I was excited.

The pilot and co-pilot were already working on their pre-flight checklist. The crew chief directed me to a seat normally reserved for a door gunner, but the machine gun had been removed. Apparently, they were expecting an uneventful flight. Boxes of miscellaneous supplies filled most of the cargo space. I have big feet, and my new jungle boots extended beyond the edge of the cargo compartment. I assumed I would have to retract my feet when the crew chief closed the door. I was wrong. The crew chief had no intention of shutting the door. The pilot added thrust to the rotors and we lifted into the air. I had been looking forward to a beautiful view through a window. Now

I was sitting on the edge of the helicopter and staring into empty space.

Helicopters are different from fixed winged planes. Planes make gentle turns; helicopters behave like sports cars. They make quick turns while steeply banking. More than once I found myself looking straight down with nothing holding me inside the helicopter except centrifugal force. I am now a firm believer in physics. The flight was over in less than fifteen minutes. As I exited the craft I looked back—I had been sitting on a safety belt!

Camp Enari was almost a small city. It was home to the 4th Inf. Division and housed several thousand people who provided support for several infantry battalions. There was also support for the support people. A large PX offered cameras, watches, clothing and an assortment of items to make life comfortable. A library offered a variety of reading material. There was even a movie theater. I found a tailor shop that offered hand-tailored suits for half the price in the states. I ordered a tan, shark-skin two-piece suit. It was sewed together in Hong Kong and delivered to my home in the states.

I was assigned to Co. C, 4th Med. Bn. Company A provided a walk-in clinic and a small infirmary for individuals residing at Camp Enari. Company B and Company C each operated clearing companies for two infantry battalions. Traditionally, each infantry battalion had an aid station, which was little more than a physician, a few medics, and a small tent. It was the first line of evacuation of the wounded. With the advent of the Med-Evac helicopters, the wounded were picked up on the battlefield and flown directly to a clearing company, where blood and other emergency supplies and treatment were available.

Since the two battalions we were supporting were deployed in the same area, only one of our clearing stations was needed. As the new kid on the block, I was assigned to the unemployed clearing station at Camp Enari. This was a safe assignment. No one at Camp Enari carried a weapon, although they could be dispensed within minutes if needed. Anyone without a job assignment was considered free labor. I spent most of my day working in the kitchen, filling sandbags or guard duty.

We had a well-fortified perimeter that allowed us to walk around the camp without weapons. I drew guard duty about once a week. It was not my favorite duty as it was always at night—I enjoyed my sleep. The perimeter consisted of three or four rows of razor-barb concertina wire with barbs as sharp as razor blades. Wires attached to trip flares stretched between the posts, which immobilized the concertina wire.

That alone should have been enough to discourage most aggressors. Men in tall towers with large search lights surveyed the area looking for any individuals who could not find the trip flares. Four or five bunkers filled the gap between the light towers. These were filled by unskilled laborers such as me.

Each bunker was dug chest-high into the ground. Double layers of sandbags formed the walls, and corrugated steel covered with sandbags completed the top. It was enough to make anyone on guard duty feel secure. A rectangular opening in the front provided sufficient room for three people to defend the perimeter, although normally only one man guarded the bunker while the other two individuals who manned the bunker slept in the bunkbeds.

Guard duty was the most despised assignment of all the "volunteer" activities. Not only did we lose sleep, but it was boring. A person can stare out at barb wire only so long before losing one's mind. We did have a field phone and could call the light tower to request a search of the area in front of the bunker. This quickly loses its appeal. The only item of true interest was the claymore mine that was left in our command. A claymore mine is the size of an opened paperback novel. A layer of buckshot in front of a sheet of C4 plastic explosive provided the lethal power. It was advertised as a directional mine, but more than one person lost his life believing this misinformation. The buckshot did project in one direction, but the mine had as much explosive power as a grenade.

The claymore mine sat menacing thirty feet in front of the bunker. It pointed outward, but a wall of sandbags behind the mine protected those of us in the bunker. Two wires from the mine extended into our bunker. All I had to do was connect the two wires to a detonator that looked like a set of pruning shears attached to a small box. If I were to squeeze the pruning shears, a pulse of electricity followed the wires to the mine causing it to explode. I spend many hours exploring how I could plausibly explode the mine accidentally.

It would have been easy to read a book by flashlight or take a catnap, but the officer of the guard made frequent visits, and he expected to be challenged before being allowed to enter the bunker. We spent more time guarding the entrance to the bunker than we did scanning the perimeter. From our viewpoint the officer of the day was a bigger threat than the North Vietnamese aggressor.

KP, guard duty, and other assorted tasks averaged a half day's work and a person can only spend so much time shopping at the PX. After a month I became bored with life. That was the least of my expectations for my tour in Vietnam. One day as I was wandering through the PX with nothing I needed to purchase I discovered a notice on a bulletin board. According to the poster it was possible to take college courses by correspondence. I could return to college while stationed in Vietnam.

I went to the company clerk to request the special form needed. He thought taking a correspondence course was a great idea, but no one had ever asked for that form before and he couldn't find it. He sent me to battalion headquarters. They thought it was a great idea, but no one had ever done it before, and they did not have the form. As Yogi Berra would say, it was déjà vu all over again. I finally found a form at division headquarters. It was the only one they had—I took it.

I signed up for *Theory of Equations* from the University of Wisconsin. I also had my parents mail my old calculus book to me. My parents thought I was going off the deep end, but I also asked them for two self-erasing drawing toys. I doubt if they still make them. They were basically a thin wax base covered with a plastic film. A stylus made the film stick to the wax creating a visible mark. When the plastic film was elevated off the wax the marks disappeared. It was great for doing homework. The military is noted for its bureaucracy. Several weeks passed and no correspondence course. I was still bored.

One morning as the company clerk was doling out assignments for the day, he asked for a volunteer. I learned early in basic training that smart people do not volunteer for anything, but no one was debating my I.Q. I did know that I would likely spend the day on K.P. or perimeter guard if I didn't volunteer. Neither of those options appealed to me. I raised my hand.

It turned out a medic was needed for a recon patrol. I would be leaving the comfort zone of base camp, but at age 20 I felt invincible. I reported for duty with a backpack filled with enough C-rations for two days, an M-16, two ammo packs attached to my belt, and six morphine syrettes. This was beginning to look serious. There were thirteen members on the patrol: ten infantrymen, a sergeant, a newly minted lieutenant and me as the medic. I felt confident in my medic skills. I hoped they were just as competent in their infantry skills.

We rode in a two and a half ton truck to our starting point. It was in the middle of nowhere. The alleged road was little more than two ruts flanked by tall bamboo shoots. I had mental visions of men with AK-47s hiding behind every bush. Just before the truck deserted us, we were each given four grenades. This was definitely not base camp. I strapped two grenades to each of my ammo packs.

We headed out in single file, with a point man walking fifty yards ahead of the rest. In theory the point man would discover any ambush before the rest of us entered the "kill" zone. Fortunately, medics were never assigned to the high-risk, point duty.

We walked through bamboo thickets, crossed open fields, and waded through small streams. The rainy season had just finished, and the weather was warm and dry. The hike through the green, rolling hills was so pleasant that I had to continuously remind myself that this was work. There could be people behind a tree or bush who would prefer me dead. The theory as explained by my companions was that recon patrols are so small that they would discover a large enemy force long before they saw us. We were to look, but not engage. I prayed their theory was accurate.

We came to a village unlike any other village I had seen in Vietnam. The living quarters were little more than circular huts made of bamboo and palm branches suspended on five-foot posts. The men of the village wore loin cloths and the women were topless. Some of the men in the patrol had not seen a female in over six months. Needless to say, there was a lot of gawking. By the time I left Vietnam ten months later, the women were beginning to cover their breasts with their hands when Americans walked through; we had taught them shame.

I learned later that these humble people were Montagnard villagers. They were indigenous people similar to American Indians and only resided in the Central Highlands. The name comes from French and means mountain people.

At the end of the day we bedded down in a bamboo thicket at the edge of a clearing. With a quarter moon, we would be able to see anyone approaching from the clearing. Anyone trying to attack from the rear would create excessive noise as they maneuvered through the bamboo. I opened one of the cans in my C-ration box and was about to eat the ham and lima beans cold when one of the regulars took pity on me. He showed me how to make a small stove by punching holes in the bottom of an empty C-ration can. He then cut off a small piece of C-4 plastic explosive from a brick he carried in his back pack for that purpose. The C-4 explodes violently when detonated by a blasting cap but otherwise hotly burns with a small blue flame. I ate warm ham and lima beans like a seasoned infantryman.

The two-day recon patrol went quickly, and I found it enjoyable. It was little more than a camping trip. The following week the company clerk asked for another volunteer. My hand went up. After that the company clerk did not ask for volunteers, but just let me know when my services were needed. These activities never made it into the letters I sent home. As far as my parents knew, I was spending my time peeling potatoes at base camp.

Despite the relaxed atmosphere of the recon patrols, they were not without danger. We never had a fire fight where we engaged the enemy, but once someone shot at a helicopter flying near our position. From the sound of the gunshot, the person shooting at the helicopter could not have been more than a hundred yards away. With the heavy foliage separating us, he could just as well have been a mile away. Another time I saw a man with an AK-47 standing in the path ahead of us. He quickly disappeared into the jungle as soon as he saw us. Perhaps he was part of a recon patrol watching us as we watched them.

One recon patrol is well etched in my memory. It was the end of the second day of a two-day patrol and the sun was beginning to set. Our second lieutenant found a good spot to bed down for the night. We had been hiking most of the day and I had to admit my feet were tired. The bivouac site offered the protection of tall bamboo stalks at our back and an open field in front. We only had to worry about aggressors coming from our front. The lieutenant created a roster of men to guard our small perimeter in one hour shifts. Medics are never assigned to "point" duty or other more hazardous tasks but that does not exclude us from guard duty. I drew third watch, which meant two hours of sleep before I was awakened.

I was well entrenched in a pleasant dream when I was shaken awake—it was my turn at guard duty. I rubbed the sleep from my eyes and reached for my M-16. I had never fired it in anger, but it was still nice knowing it was there. Someone in the dark handed me the field radio. It would be my job to babysit with the radio for the next hour. The radio was our only contact with the outside world. If we were attacked, all I had to do was announce it on the radio and within minutes we would have helicopter gunships circling overhead. Our second lieutenant had given our coordinates to basecamp. I wondered how well our lieutenant scored in map reading during his OCS training.

I leaned back against a bamboo stalk the diameter of a small tree trunk and looked out at the beauty before me. There was no moon on a cloudless night. I had seen star-filled skies before, but nothing compared to what was now displayed before me. Only the largest cities in Vietnam had street lights and billboards, and we were bivouacked in the middle of nowhere. Light pollution was non-existent. I stared up at the endless stars that seemed to go on forever. It made me feel insignificant. I was only one person on a planet that was meaningless compared to the eternal universe. It was a humbling experience.

The multitude of stars also made me feel lonely. People back home would wonder how I could be lonely when I had twelve close friends sleeping beside me. Most of them I had met on previous recon patrols, but I knew only a few by real names. Most of them had nicknames like Tex or Spider. I would give my life for them as they would for me. War is not about a philosophy. Soldiers fight for their buddy in the foxhole beside them and not for patriotism.

I looked across the field wondering if the enemy who we called Charlie was prowling around. This was the time of night when they liked to shoot rockets at our base camp. There was mostly dead silence, not even crickets chirping. Occasionally, I would hear a noise in front of me, but there are many animals other than Charlie that can make noise in the night. Shadows in the distance appeared to move. I wondered if it were my imagination. Auto-kinesis can make shadows appear to move in the dark. I compared the distance between shadows as I had been taught. It didn't change; it had to be my imagination.

Moments later a ribbon of light waved across the sky. The ribbon was red in color and appeared to be on fire. This was soon followed by a deep moaning sound that confirmed my suspicions. The Air Force calls them AC-47s, but people on the ground below call them Puff the Magic Dragon or Spooky. They are twin-engine planes equipped with three mini-guns each capable of spitting out 6,000 rounds a minute. The tracer rounds fire so close together that it appears as a ribbon of red light and the sound blends into a mournful moan. It was actually a pretty display until I thought of the people below who might be dying. It reminded me of the song *They Call the Wind Maria* from the musical *Paint Your Wagon.* "Maria makes the mountains sound like folks were out there dying." Puff circled around our position spewing out its deadly ribbon of fire. It never came closer than a quarter mile to our position. I wondered how accurate the coordinates were that the lieutenant gave to base camp.

Soon after Puff left the 105 howitzers on top of Dragon Mountain near base camp opened up. The exploding shells circled our position. Fortunately, they left more space between us than Puff did. The noise was unsettling, at least for me. No one else woke up. Apparently, someone in the chain of command thought we were in danger. I never heard any more about it. The shells were still exploding when I awoke my relief. He did not seem concerned. I wrapped myself in my poncho liner and quickly fell asleep. Years later I wrote a short story based on this recon patrol. It was a work of fiction, but eighty percent of it was based on fact. I called the short story *Silent Night.*

18

Silent Night
A Short Story

Spider touches my shoulder and instantly I am awake. "It's two o'clock," he says.

I flick on my flashlight under my poncho and look at my watch. The watch's dial under the red light confirms the time. It is not that I do not trust him, but it feels like I had just gotten to sleep. My turn at watch is from two to three; after which, I can return to sleep.

"Is anything going on?" I ask in a low whisper.

"No," he says, "Nothing unusual."

"Did you do the radio check?"

"No."

Spider is wrapping himself in his poncho liner, showing no intention of making the call. I place the radio's receiver up to my ear and key the mike.

"Sawbones 83 to Deadwood." I wait for a reply.

"Sawbones 83, this is Deadwood. Go ahead. Over."

"Sawbones 83 to Deadwood. How do you read us? Over."

"I read you lima charlie (loud and clear). Over."

"Sawbones 83…out."

I lean back against the trunk of a large bamboo tree and stare out at the darkness. Behind me is a large bamboo forest with stalks rising up like thick prison bars. With a sharp machete one might make fifty feet an hour. If they come they must come from the front where the land had once been cleared for farming. It has since been reclaimed by tall grass.

Spider is already breathing deeply in the early stages of sleep. War teaches one how to master sleep. Tonight I sleep in the grass at the edge of a bamboo thicket; two months ago it had been up against the still-warm foundation of a burned out schoolhouse in downtown Pleiku—compliments of the Tet offensive.

I again stare into the darkness. Anything beyond ten feet is no more than a shadow. My mind drifts off to the real world. It is exactly twelve hours away. At home it is also two o'clock. My father will be at work. My mother might be working today as a waitress at a local diner if it is not her day off. I have a brother in the Peace Corps in Panama. There is no telling what he might be doing. Loneliness begins to set in.

"How can I be lonely with so many people around me?" you ask. "They are my friends," you say.

I am forced to acknowledge the wisdom of your argument. Around me are ten infantrymen, a sergeant, and a newly minted second lieutenant. They are my friends. People back home assume we are fighting for our country—out of patriotism. What we fight for, when the bullets begin to fly, is not patriotism; it is for the guy in the foxhole beside us. That is what we fight for. It's as simple as that—nothing more. I will offer my life for the people beside me, as they will for me. Two days ago, before the recon patrol had begun, we had been strangers. I didn't even know their names. Now I do. One is named Spider, one is Juice, and we have a Tex. Every unit has a Tex. No matter what name I might have offered for myself, my name would be Doc. I am their medic. Those are all the names we need to know. Anything more is superfluous.

Perhaps loneliness is not the best term to express my feelings. Perhaps it is deeper than that—more a feeling of insignificance. I look above me. In the gap of the bamboo shoots I see a portion of the sky with its endless stars. The cleared area on the ground in front of me seems to zoom out like a cheap Hollywood movie stunt. It soon disappears, and the globe of the earth materializes. That too becomes smaller as the camera continues its outward zoom until the earth is only a speck, a small blue dot in some inconspicuous corner of the universe. I can now see myself from the viewpoint of the stars that have been shining down on earth for eternity.

"In the realm of the endless and eternal universe…do you believe a man sitting at the edge of a clearing with an M-16 in his lap, praying he will see the light of another sunrise, really makes a difference?" the stars ask.

I can offer no reply.

In the sky that hangs loosely over the clearing in front of me are more stars. One of them is moving toward me. It has to be a plane or helicopter. At this time of night, it is more likely the former. About a mile south of me, it begins to circle. I see the glowing, orange ribbon first. It looks like a streamer of crepe paper someone is waving in the nighttime sky. But the fiery brilliance is breathtaking. Seconds later the sound reaches my ears. It is a low moan.

The Air Force calls them AC-47s, twin-engine planes equipped with three mini-guns each capable of spitting out 6,000 rounds a minute. Those of us unfortunate enough to have seen them in action from the ground looking up called them "Spooky" or "Puff the Magic Dragon."

I watch the plane circle around spitting out its tracer fire. On the last round, it comes within 1,000 yards of our position. I key the mike on our radio.

"Sawbones 83 to Deadwood, over."

"Sawbones 83, this is Deadwood. Go ahead, over."

"Be advised we have a Spooky at our front door. Does he know we are here? Does he have our coordinates? Over."

"Wait one, Sawbones 83…"

I visualize Deadwood back at base camp with his feet upon some desk. He will have a cup of coffee in his left hand and will now be reaching for a sandwich with his right. After he has taken a couple of bites, he will pick up the landline and place a call to whoever is in charge of Spooky. It might not be fair, but that is the image lodged in my mind.

"Sawbones 83, this is Deadwood. Over."

"Deadwood, this is Sawbones 83. We're still here. We're not going anywhere."

"Be advised that S-2 (military intelligence) has reason to believe Charlie is in your sector. Spooky is there in your honor. When he leaves they might place some H and I rounds (harassment and interdiction) around your perimeter to keep Charlie honest."

"Roger that, Deadwood. Sawbones 83, out."

I hope my voice sounded calm and professional over the radio. It is not the way I feel. One small error and Spooky will be raining bullets down upon us like a summer hailstorm. Friendly fire won't even earn a purple heart. Does a wound from friendly fire hurt less? I wonder how well our lieutenant scored in his map-reading class at OCS.

I wait in the darkness, watching Puff do her thing. The ribbons of fire created by the tracers are almost a work of art as they lace through the nighttime sky. The moaning sound is unsettling, sending a chill through my body. It reminds me of the song *They Call the Wind Maria* from the musical *Paint Your Wagon*. How does that verse go?... "Maria makes the mountains sound like folks was out there dying."

Is someone out there dying under that deluge of gunfire? I wonder. Maybe no one will ever know.

"If someone in a woods cries out in pain and there is no one there to hear his cry, does he still suffer in pain?" I ask.

"That's stupid," I reply. "The pain is just as real."

"Must you two always bicker?" a third voice says.

"Yes, we must," they reply in unison.

They are both right, of course—each in his own way. Somewhere, as I sit here in the dark, a woman is being raped. Not a sensual sex act, but a brutal, violent attack that is every bit as traumatic as anything this war has to offer. Somewhere, there is a young child suffering pain from the terminal stages of cancer.   Somewhere, there is a mother or wife receiving a notice from a military chaplain.   But I do not know them; therefore, they do not exist. They never happened.

"That is precisely the point I was trying to make," I say.

"But it's still real to the people involved," I reply.

It is obvious those two are not about to give it a rest. I don't know why I put up with them. Spider doesn't suffer from these kinds of conflicts. He described his hour as "nothing unusual."

I lay my gun on the ground and reach into my rucksack for the remains of my dinner. It is a can of ham and lima beans from the C-ration pack. It has no commercial value, as it cannot be traded for anything. It is literally the bottom of the food chain. When you're hungry, you'll eat anything. I open the can with my P-38 can opener and scoop out the contents with my plastic spoon. It isn't the tastiest meal, but it does give me something to do and keeps my mind from wandering.

I finish the beans with a polite, but subdued, burp and toss the can to the side. It will have to be picked up in the morning— nothing will be left to confirm our existence. But then it will be daylight. We will be able to see what we are doing.

I reach out with my right hand for my M-16—it isn't there. I am overtaken with panic. My heart races within my chest. I begin to hyperventilate. With both hands I begin patting the ground. It only takes a moment or two to find the gun, but my heart continues to race. I hold it close to my chest. I don't know why. My gun is still a virgin. It has never been fired in anger. Hopefully, it never will. Every time the fecal matter hits the proverbial fan, a medic is too busy to need a gun. Still, it is my security blanket and I need it. I even have dreams at night about losing my gun. Some people have dreams about having no clothes. I have dreams of having no gun. I am sure other people do not share such dreams. Sometimes I worry about my mental stability. Even emotionally stable people have been known to crack during wartime.

I clutch my gun to my chest like a mother clutching an infant just rescued from perilous danger; then I feel foolish. I pull my poncho over my head and turn on my flashlight: it is two-thirty. My watch is half done.

I stare out at the darkness for another ten minutes. In the darkness, there is nothing to see. With no wind, there is nothing to hear. Except for the lingering smell of ham and lima beans, there is nothing to smell. A university psychology department could not have constructed a better sensory-deprivation lab. It is good, but not perfect. About every five minutes, an artillery shell falls around our perimeter. They do provide more personal space than Spooky did. None of them fall closer to us than half a mile. No one in our squad is even awakened.

Those noises I can overlook. Those noises I can understand. What is disconcerting are the occasional noises coming from in front of me. They are subtle to be sure, perhaps just my imagination. A lonely watch can do that to you. If someone else were present, the noise would qualify for a "Did you hear that?" Nothing more.

Sometimes the noises are real. That does not necessarily make them sinister. Every land has its share of wildlife capable of making noises in the night. I stare more closely at the shadows in the distance—they appear to be moving. I rub my eyes and look again. Sometimes when there is no background for reference, objects can appear to move. It is called auto-kinesis. The shadows continue to move. I focus on two shadows, paying attention mostly to the space between them—this appears constant. It is probably my imagination.

On the practical side, it would make no difference if they were real or imaginary. We are a recon team. We are to avoid contact at all costs. We are not moving and are making no noise. We have the trees to our back, eliminating any visible shadows. We will see them long before they will see us.

What would happen if I did come face-to-face with my counterpart? Would I hesitate? Would he hesitate? Our country has been in many wars. All of our enemies are now our friends. Can I kill a man tonight who tomorrow could have been my friend? If I were to pretend I don't see him, would he pretend he doesn't see me and walk away?

I push my thoughts into the far recesses of my brain, but they are like articles of clothing in an over-stuffed suitcase—they resist closure.

I remain in place with my back resting against the bamboo backrest, giving the chimerical bogey the right of passage. The next fifteen minutes are uneventful. I again crawl under my poncho to check the time: It is now five minutes to three; my watch is almost over. I key the mike on the radio. It is time for our hourly radio check.

"Sawbones 83 to Deadwood." There is no answer.

"Sawbones 83 to Deadwood." I again wait for a reply.

"Sawbones 83, this is Deadwood. Go ahead, over."

I can hear radio music in the background. Deadwood obviously does not get as much fresh air as we do.

"Sawbones 83 to Deadwood, how do you read us, over?"

"I read you lima charlie, over."

"Sawbones 83, out."

It should now be three o'clock. I crawl over to Juice and touch him on the shoulder. He is instantly awake.

"It's three o'clock…time for your shift," I whisper.

Juice rubs his eyes in hopes it will help him see into the darkness: it does not.

"Anything happen on your shift?" he asks.

"Same-O, Same-O," I reply, "Nothing unusual."

19

Fire Base Oasis

Unbeknown to me a drama was playing out at the Oasis Fire Base where Charlie Company maintained a clearing station. The clearing station normally had two physicians, eight to ten medics, and a lab tech. The current lab tech was obnoxious and irritating. He did nothing worthy of a court martial, but the physicians sent word to company headquarters that he had to go before someone killed him. They needed a replacement. Military lab techs have an additional year of training beyond the basic medic training, and we had no such replacements within the company. I didn't know what the lab tech did to irritate the physicians, but they were adamant about his needed departure and were willing to settle for anyone capable of diagnosing gonorrhea and malaria. They were the two major medical problems confronting soldiers in Vietnam.

During a Monday morning roll call, I was informed the company commander wished to speak to me—that is never a good omen. I normally kept a low profile and wondered where I had screwed up. I entered Captain Edwards' office with hat in hand and saluted as required. Captain Edwards motioned for me to take a seat. He shuffled some papers before he gave me his full attention. He stood over six feet three inches and would have been intimidating even without his captain's bars. He looked me up and down, making me wish I had polished my boots and brass belt buckle.

"The company clerk says you're interested in learning."

It was a statement but sounded more like a question. The clerk must have informed the commander that I had depleted the division's entire supply of correspondence course applications. I was mulling over how best to apologize, when he asked if I would be willing to learn a few simple lab exams and replace the lab tech at the forward clearing station. He didn't need to ask twice. I would be transferred closer to the front, but I would be spending my time looking through a microscope. My background was in math and the physical sciences, but I did like biology.

The following Monday I reported to the lab at Alpha Company. They provided routine care for individuals stationed at base camp. I was expecting a well-equipped lab with incubators and rows of cupboards filled with pipettes, Pyrex flasks, and other glassware. What I discovered was a small room with microscope and centrifuge resting on a table top. It was a one-man operation. I wish I could remember the man's name, for he was a great teacher.

He started me off mixing gram stains. That was chemistry. I was in my element. A gram stain consists of a series of solutions that stain bacteria. If the bacteria stain blue they are considered gram positive. If the bacteria stain pink they are called gram negative. This is an important distinction when diagnosing gonorrhea. After a penile discharge is gram stained, it is viewed under the microscope. The gonorrhea bacteria are gram negative, intracellular diplococci. I would search under the microscope for two kidney-bean shaped bacteria clinging together, and then compared it to a textbook picture of gonorrhea. I mastered the gonorrhea exam by the end of the day.

Diagnosing malaria was more difficult but far more interesting. We used Giemsa stain for this procedure. To make the slide I placed a drop of blood on a slide and then slid a second slide across the first slide to create a thin film of blood with feathered edges. The trick was to make a blood smear that was one cell thick. We fixed the slide in alcohol to adhere the blood to the slide and then dipped the slide into the Giemsa stain. Giemsa-stained blood is pure beauty when viewed under a microscope. White cells offered nuclei in a variety of artistic shapes and colors. I could spend hours scanning a blood smear, but this was work and I had to focus on finding parasites. What I was looking for were malaria parasites attached to red cells. The parasites formed round pink rings with a bright red nucleus on the rim of the ring. The malaria parasites were rare, and it took many minutes of scanning the red cells before conceding that the parasites were not present. After two weeks I was pronounced an expert in diagnosing malaria and gonorrhea. I was ready to head toward the combat zone. The following day I caught a ride to Firebase Oasis.

Firebase Oasis was first established in 1965 by the 1st Cavalry Division, but was later turned over to the 4th Inf. Div. The firebase was located fifteen miles southwest of Pleiku and close to the Cambodian border. Cambodia was home to the Ho Chi Minh Trail used by the North Vietnamese to resupply their troops. That made it important real estate. The artillery battalion stationed at the Oasis could cover most of the area up to the Cambodian border. The Oasis was also the supply depot for the 2nd Brigade. The firebase was smaller than our base at Camp Enari, but it was still a large operation.

Our clearing station sat in the middle of the Oasis next to a helicopter landing pad. An 18 X 52 foot GP Large tent housed our emergency and triage room. Numerous stretchers on metal saw horses occupied one side of the tent, and large containers holding medications, surgical instruments, and bandages filled the other side. A heavy duty electrical cord running down the center of the tent provided electricity. We had a noisy generator located behind the tent that kept our lights going twenty-four hours a day. It also kept our refrigerator with O negative blood cold. O negative blood is considered the universal donor and can be given to anyone without fear of rejection. We seldom had time or resources to type and match blood on dying patients.

A smaller 16 X 32 foot GP Medium tent housed our inpatient unit. This tent was only wide enough for a single row of cots. A small desk for the "nurse's" station occupied the front of the tent. I placed "nurse's" in quotations because we had no nurses. Our staff consisted of a dentist, two doctors, and about eight to ten medics. My laboratory table and equipment filled the area across from the nurse's station.

A third tent (GP Large) provided sleeping quarters for everyone except for the officers who slept in a six-sided GP Small tent. Our living conditions were rugged, but I have camped with less amenities. We slept on cots with overhanging mosquito netting. We were required to take a daily antimalarial pill for one species of malaria and a weekly pill to protect us from a second species.

We erected the three tents perpendicular to each other like spokes on a wheel. If the inpatient tent was pointing north, the triage tent would be pointing west and the barracks tent would be pointing east. A small parachute covered the hub of the wheel. During the rainy season, it was possible to walk from one tent to the next without getting soaked. A double-width, chest-high, sandbag wall surrounded all tents. As far as I can remember, the sandbag wall was never challenged while I was at the Oasis.

We received casualties once or twice a week on average. We dressed wounds, splinted fractures, and started IVs. Sometimes we just filled body bags. No one questioned the politics of the Vietnam War. People would die without our help. That was all the motivation we needed. We stabilized the casualties and then med-evaced them to the 71st Evac Hospital within three or four hours. It was all part of the job.

Not all casualties were Americans. Occasionally we received North Vietnamese prisoners. The Geneva Convention dictated that prisoners of war shall receive the same quality of medical care. We followed those rules religiously. There was also an unwritten rule that we should not coddle POWs. The rational was that terrified POWs are more likely to provide military intelligence. One day we had a POW that must have been in his early teens. I don't think he was even wounded. He was sitting on a stretcher that straddled two metal saw horses. He looked petrified. I was sure he had heard horrifying rumors about us as we had heard about them. I poured some M & M's onto his hand and then took one of them and ate it to prove they were safe. I had never seen anyone previously show compassion to a POW, but many medics saw my actions. Compassion for POWs became the new norm. Sometimes small acts of kindness can change the world.

The Oasis was home to many support groups, which required a fair amount of labor. The army outsourced the simpler jobs to highly vetted Vietnamese workers. It was not unusual to see them inside the perimeter during daylight hours, but they were expected to leave the compound before dark. One eight year old boy appeared to have adopted our clearing station. We were his de facto daycare center while his mother or other family member worked. We called him Little John. He spoke excellent English and was quite popular. Having an eight year old hanging around reminded people of home and family. Little John did have one flaw—we couldn't trust him. Anything not nailed down ended up inside his pockets. We routinely frisked him before he left our area. I am sure it was a survival skill on his part. We had endless riches and he had little. Little John was particularly interested in my lab. He enjoyed looking through the microscope. I taught him how to use the hand-cranked centrifuge, but most of the other lab skills were above his level.

One day Little John arrived with his little brother in tow. I find it difficult to judge Vietnamese children, but he appeared no more than four. He was obviously sick with a high fever. We frequently treated the local Vietnamese, so with little discussion the doctors admitted Little John's brother to our inpatient unit. Malaria is the most common cause of high fever, but I needed confirmation. I poked the young brother's finger to obtain some blood—he didn't even flinch.

I fixed the blood smear with alcohol to make it adhere to the slide and then stained it with Giemsa. Then I placed it under my microscope and dialed up the high power. Normally, it requires five or ten minutes of searching before I find a red cell with a malarial parasite. This was not the case with Little John's brother. I found dozens of parasites in one field of view. At least forty percent of the red cells were infected. Closer exam revealed the cells were infected with both P. falciparum and P. vivax. They were the most common species of malaria in Vietnam. I had never seen both species in the same patient. It did not look good.

With the diagnoses in hand, the physicians began the appropriate medication. Because the infection was so advanced, the physicians decided Little John's brother should remain in the ward tent. I set up a cot for Little John next to his brother. We treated our patient with around the clock Tylenol to keep his fever down, but it still spiked as high as one hundred and five. It would take a day or two before the antimalarial medicine took effect. Our patient was holding his own when I bid Little John and him good night. I headed to our barracks tent

The following morning I headed for the ward tent to see how our patient was doing, but I was stopped by one of the physicians. Little John was still sleeping, and the doctor did not want him disturbed—his brother had died during the night.

I had become inured to the death of war, but young children should not die. Not from a killer that can only be seen through a microscope. I returned to my cot with tears in my eyes. I didn't want to be around when the physicians told Little John of his brother's death. That may have been cowardly of me, but I could not find the words to express my grief. He had entrusted his brother to us, and we had failed.

I polished my boots, which was a useless gesture. In the rainy season the boots are always covered with mud and in the dry season they are covered with dust. I wondered if I would ever see Little John again. I didn't need to wait long to find out. Little John was seeking me out. After he found me he shook my hand and thanked me for caring for his brother. Neither of us had dry eyes. I later discovered he sought out everyone who had cared for his brother to thank them.

We offered Little John a body bag or blanket to cover his brother, but he declined. Any other time he would have gladly stolen the blanket. He picked up his brother and walked back to his village. I assumed that would be the last we would see of him, but two days later he returned with his mother and another sibling. They tested positive for malaria. The mother also had tuberculosis. The physicians started them on medicine and arranged for long-term care. I wished them well.

After two months at the Oasis the infantry battalions were on the move, and we needed to follow them. Our tents and medical equipment were too heavy and bulky for air transport. That meant a convoy. In driver's training in high school, we were taught on a car with a stick shift. The theory was we would be able to drive anything. Other schools did not share that philosophy, and few medics knew how to use a clutch. I was, therefore, given command of a two and a half ton truck. It had multi-wheel drive and drove more like a tank than a sports car.

The officer in charge of the convoy placed our cracker-box ambulance and two trucks toward the rear of the convoy where we would less likely be involved in an ambush and could better offer support to those who were. At the very rear was a heavy-duty tow truck capable of rescuing any vehicles with mechanical problems.

If there were paved roads in Vietnam, I never found them. The better roads were gravel while the rest were dirt packed by many traveling vehicles. Fortunately, my truck had a high clearance. I could easily drive over protruding rocks. Many times we were flanked by jungle on both sides. If we were to be ambushed the outcome would be little different than that of the Redcoats at Lexington and Concord. We were instructed to keep moving if at all possible during an ambush to escape the ambush zone. If the vehicle should become incapacitated, we were to evacuate the vehicle as soon as possible and take cover at the road edge. I was to go to the left side of the road and my "shotgun" would head for the right side of the road.

I have never been ambushed while driving in a convoy, but I did see a wall of large rocks blocking the right side of the road once. It was a man-made obstacle that my truck was incapable of driving over. I felt my heart sink in my chest, and I expected to see bullets coming through my windshield at any moment. The left lane was open, so I stepped on the gas and ran through more gears than I think the truck possessed. I was able to swerve around the rock barricade without tipping over the truck. I didn't start breathing again until we were one hundred yards farther down the road. Apparently, the ambush site was from another day. No one found it necessary to clear both sides of the road. The experience was still sufficient to require many of us to change underwear.

Setting up a clearing station at a new fire base was never fun. Not only did we have to set up the large tents and unpack the equipment, but we had to fill sandbags two layers deep and chest high around all the tents and around the front of our vehicles. It took ten days or more before we could slack off. During this time we still treated casualties as they occurred.

20

Thanksgiving

We moved frequently during the fall of 1967. Every two or three weeks we loaded our tents and supplies into the back of our two and a half ton trucks and headed to a new location. The war didn't stop just because we were in transit to a new location. We equipped our cracker box ambulance with bandages, IV solutions, and other emergency equipment. Our blood supply was packed in ice on one of the trucks and stored within easy reach. We were capable of opening up our shop with a five minutes notice. Fortunately, we were never tested while on convoy. The Med-Evac helicopters knew our limitations and flew patients directly to the 71st Evac hospital.

Most of the temporary fire bases were small with little more than a company of 105mm howitzers, perhaps some maintenance people, and us. The howitzers made noisy neighbors. They fired periodically throughout the night. Everyone lived in villages, and anyone outside the villages at night was assumed to be up to no good. The howitzers randomly harassed those positions to keep everyone honest. This made sleeping difficult, but I soon learned to differentiate between outgoing rounds and an incoming rocket explosion. The gunpowder inside the howitzer had to entirely burn before the projectile left the muzzle. This created a rapid boom. Incoming rockets and mortars did not have this constraint, and the noise was longer in duration. After a couple of weeks I learned to sleep through the out-going rounds, but instinctively rolled off my cot if I heard rocket fire.

Medics don't normally pull perimeter guard, but people with more rank than I overlooked this limitation when the firebase had limited personal. One Wednesday I drew the short straw and was assigned to twenty-four hour guard duty. A man from the maintenance company and I were given a two-man foxhole to defend. The foxhole was waist deep, which allowed us to sit on the ground at the rear of the hole and dangle our feet over the edge. A semicircle of double-wide sandbags in front of the hole provided protection up to our armpits if we were to stand in the hole.

It is impossible to describe how boring guard duty can be; one can only share so much with a guard partner. After little more than an hour, we each knew the other's entire life history. While sitting on the back rim of our foxhole I noticed one of the sandbags appeared loose and out of alignment. Normally we flatten the sandbags with a large wooden mallet. The sandbag in question was still fluffy. I am not a perfectionist, but after a few hours of boredom this became a major affront to my sense of world order.

I lifted the sandbag with the intention of correcting this malalignment and discovered the reason for the disorderly sandbag—someone left a paperback under the sandbag. I lost all interest in the sandbag; I had a book! I didn't care about the title or genre. It was something to read the rest of the day. Guard duty was no longer a tedious assignment.

The pages were well-worn but readable. I assumed many people had read it before me. I read the title on the cover: *Salute to Sandy*. I hadn't heard of this title, but the author was a household name. Dale Evans and her husband Roy Rogers had a highly successful TV show from 1951-1957. Westerns were big in those days.

The book was about their adopted son Sandy Rogers. Sandy was severely beaten by his biological father. When he was adopted by Roy Rogers and Dale Evens, he had significant brain damage as well as rickets from malnutrition. He did poorly in school. While visiting Hawaii, Sandy fell in love with the marines. Joining the military became his life ambition. Sandy volunteered at the local Army recruiting station. His parents assumed he would be rejected because of his physical and mental disabilities, but in those days the army was taking anyone with a pulse. He was still found unqualified for Vietnam and sent to Germany. When he was promoted to Private First Class he attended a drinking party where his "friends" encouraged him to drink like a man. He overdosed on alcohol and died at a local hospital.

I finished the book at dusk. I placed the book under the sandbag, being careful to leave the sandbag misaligned. I wondered how many other people would read the book.

I opened my C-ration box to see what I had in store for dinner. It was a three-course dinner as I expected. I was pleased to find the main entrée was Beef Slices w/ Potatoes in Gravy. I could have done worse. Another can contained four hardtack biscuits, which most people called John Wayne cookies. They were not so bad once they were slathered with the cheese spread or peanut butter that accompanied the cookies. The last can contained sliced peaches. My foxhole buddy was stuck with a can of ham and lima beans. He offered to trade. I laughed at his suggestion. Neither meal was worthy of the time required to open the cans with our P-38 can openers. Tomorrow would be different. It was Thanksgiving, and we were promised a full turkey and dressing dinner to celebrate the occasion. The meal would be served on metal trays, but turkey is still turkey.

We had a 24 hour shift, so no turkey until the sun rose in the morning. We still had eight hours of darkness before us. We flipped a coin to see who got the coveted first four-hour shift. I lost and got the 2 to 6 a.m. shift. I find it easier to stay awake for the first four hours. Trying to stay awake after being awoken from a deep sleep can be challenging.

I lay down and used my folded poncho for a pillow. It wasn't comfortable, but Uncle Sam was not paying us the big bucks to be comfortable. I fell asleep only to be awoken by the occasional aerial flare that changed blackness to bright daylight as quickly as flipping a switch. The flares lasted less than thirty seconds, but it was sufficient to ruin a good dream.

My foxhole partner woke me precisely at 2 a.m. I was about to challenge him on his timing until I checked my watch; it was 2 a.m. I stood up to stretch before beginning my watch. I questioned the value of our guard duty. It was so dark I would not be capable of seeing our adversary before he was close enough to shake his hand. Then an aerial flare exploded two hundred yards over our heads. A canister of burning magnesium swung below a large parachute. They were usually fired from a mortar. The 105 howitzers were capable of firing flares, but they couldn't shoot straight up. The current flare was courtesy of a mortar somewhere within the compound. I scanned the land in front of us; nothing moved. The North Vietnamese seldom attacked at night. They preferred first daylight. At least that is what I had been told.

The occasional flares helped me stay awake. Time seemed to drag. I was tempted to shake my watch to see if was still working. Finally I saw light in the east; my twenty-four hour guard duty was almost over. I watched as the morning light illuminated the open field in front of our foxhole. It looked no different than it did when the sun set the previous evening.

A flash of light two hundred yards in front of our foxhole caught my attention. A moment later I heard the blast; it was an incoming mortar round. A quick scan revealed no approaching soldiers. It was only a mortar attack, but mortar attacks can be deadly. Another round exploded fifty yards closer than the first. It is easy to point a mortar at the intended target, but adjusting for distance is mostly guesswork without accurate coordinates.

It was common to gradually lower the elevation of the mortar tube and "walk" the rounds toward the intended target.

I did not time the explosions, but my best guess was they were fifteen seconds apart. Each round exploded fifty yards closer to our foxhole. They were coming straight toward us. If my calculations were accurate the next round would fall right on us. We crouched as low as we could in our foxhole. We couldn't abandon our post even if there was a better shelter to run to.

We waited for the next round to explode. Sometimes fifteen seconds can seem like eternity. We waited—and we waited. But no other rounds exploded. I don't know if they ran out of mortar rounds or perhaps they were in a hurry to evacuate the area before gunships arrived. I will never know the reason for our survival, but I did know it was November 28, 1967, Thanksgiving morning.

21

Ban Blech

Late December found us on the outskirts of a small village called Ban Blech. This firebase had more to offer than many of our previous locations, and it was rumored we would stay for a while. Moving to a new location involved excessive work and sleepless nights. It was imperative that all our tents had a waist-high, double-thick row of sandbags. We had no desire to repeat this effort every two weeks. Since this was a well-established firebase, we were able to commandeer sandbags from the previous tenants. We placed our tents next to the hard-packed airstrip. The airstrip was only certified for small cargo planes and helicopters, but it was a perfect location to receive incoming casualties.

Treating the sick and wounded was the reason for our existence, but many times our patients died before their arrival at our aid station. Vietnam was hot and we didn't have a morgue. The best we could do was place the dead bodies in green body bags that sealed in fluids and odors. It was not a popular duty. Most of the time the bodies were identified in the field and arrived with an appropriate toe tag. Each soldier also wore a dog tag with name and blood type. When in doubt, the bodies were flown to Hawaii for further identification. With dental records and DNA from tissue samples, everyone was eventually identified.

One afternoon an armored personnel carrier caught fire. I no longer remember the cause, but it burned for several days, and no one could get near the APC because of the ammunition erratically cooking off. We had no way to save the individuals trapped inside. Once the APC cooled off, we placed the charred bodies into body bags. With their dog tags and dental records, graves registration would quickly identify the bodies and send the remains back to family members for tearful funerals. It was a grim ritual.

Ten days later when the APC was being prepared for disposal, another body part was discovered. A medic named John Griffin and I were on duty when they brought in a short piece of femur surrounded by what looked like charcoal. The correct course of action was to package the charred femur and send it to Hawaii for identification. Heat destroys DNA and the femur did not come with dental records or dog tag. Graves Registration would identify the body part by looking for missing body parts from the previously processed bodies. Eventually they would forward the femur to family members who had already held a memorial service for their loved one and buried the remains.

After a short discussion, John and I decided the family did not deserve further grief. It may not have been proper or ethical, but John and I buried the femur behind our clearing station. The soldier's family would not receive body parts of their beloved soldier piece by piece.

I didn't know what happened to the bodies of North Vietnamese soldiers when they were killed. If their comrades retrieved the bodies, there was no simple way to return them to North Vietnam. I assumed they were left on the battlefield or buried on the spot. Once a Long Range Recon Patrol (LRRP) dragged a body into our aid station. They had been criticized for their high "body count" and wanted to provide proof. It was not what we wanted, and we were not happy. No one knew what to do with the body. It became another body I helped bury. We covered the deceased's face with cloth, so we would not throw dirt directly on his face. I considered reciting the Lord's Prayer, but decided that would not be appropriate as he was most likely Buddhist. Back in North Vietnam, he would be listed as missing in action. His family would never have closure.

Most of the time we received ample warning of incoming casualties. Sometimes it was just a notification of contact with the enemy. Other times we had the actual number of injured and type of injuries. Once we received a radio report from a gunship helicopter. Their door gunner had been shot in the head, and they were three minutes out. I could already see the helicopter in the distance. I grabbed my aid bag and ran toward the air strip. I assumed others would follow with a stretcher. The crew chief had removed the door gunner's helmet, and I could see the back of the door gunner's head. It was a distorted mixture of bone and brain tissue. He was talking in incoherent phrases, but nothing made sense. I stabilized the head and neck while other medics placed him on a stretcher.

We were a hundred yards from our ER tent. I assumed people were preparing IVs, oxygen, and other appropriate equipment. It was a hot day, but we still ran the entire way. Four medics carried the stretcher feet first, while I tried my best to stabilize the shattered head as we ran. By the time we reached the ER tent, the patient's incoherent phrases had deteriorated to garbled words, and then silence.

I am not a runner. It was a hot day, and I was exhausted and thirsty. The physicians were now in charge, and there was nothing further I could do. I walked over to the water tank to quench my thirst. I cupped my hands under the tap to catch the flowing water. It tasted salty. I stared down at my cupped hands—they were covered with brain tissue mixed with blood. I had eaten someone's brain. Technically, that made me a cannibal. It should have been a revolting experience, but it wasn't. It was part of the job. I was more shocked by my lack of emotion. What kind of person can eat brain tissue and not find it revolting? I wondered if I could ever return to normal society.

We kept the patient alive long enough to Med-Evac him to the 71st Evac Hospital, where I am sure he died. I have looked at the Vietnam Wall on several occasions. I knew his name was somewhere on the wall, but I didn't know where. Many patients have died in my arms, but his death is the one that haunts me the most. Every time I bite my lip or taste blood I think of him. I am not a poet but I did write one poem more for me than anyone else. It is in his honor.

I have been to the Wall
and have touched the cold granite.
Bleak in its blackness
on the mall it does stand
reminding us of the men
who died in that far away land.

I have been to the Wall
in search of a friend
who, in the prime of his life,
answered the call,
his name etched in granite
there on the Wall.

I know not his name
nor does he mine
fore we met but a moment
in that far away land,
two ships in the night
both answered the call,
but his name alone
is etched on the Wall.

Does anyone remember
that carefree young man
snatched from our midst
in that far away land?

Does anyone remember
who knelt by his side,
who fought back the tears
the day that he died?

Does anyone remember
the hands drenched in blood
that cradled his head
as his life ebbed away,
there in the mud
on the ground where he lay?

Does anyone remember
that carefree young man
snatched from our midst
in that far away land?

I do.
Larry Buege Medic, 4th Infantry Div. 1967-68

December was in the middle of Vietnam's dry season It had been several months since I had last experienced rain. The ground was covered with dust, and so were we. Any gust of wind sent a blanket of dust swirling in the air. Sometimes we had dust tornadoes or what some people call dust devils. They didn't have the wind speed of a regular tornado, but they could cause serious eye damage if googles were not worn. To reduce dust in our barracks tent, we covered the dirt floor with old wooden pallets. In theory the dust would settle through the cracks in the boards and eliminate stirring up the dust when walking through the tent. It provided mixed results.

We set our tents in the normal 9, 12, and 3 o'clock position. Since we expected to stay for an extended time, the section sergeant asked us to find a parachute we could place over the junction of the three tents to reduce dust and provide relief from the sun. I teamed up with a guy who was good at "midnight requisitions." Everything belonged to the military. As long as equipment was re-purposed for military use, it was not considered stealing. Radar O'Reilly of M.A.S.H. fame would understand. I was his technical assistant. My friend requisitioned a large aerial flare, the type normally dropped from an airplane. The trick was to remove the large parachute without triggering the explosive charge or igniting the magnesium used for illumination. I like to think it was skill, but perhaps a lot of it was luck. I managed to snip the proper wires and remove the correct screws. We soon had a large parachute to shelter the junction of the three tents. We buried the remains of the flare, so it would not harm anyone.

We stacked a few crates to make a primitive bar and our canteen was in business. Drinking alcohol while on duty or before five was prohibited, but other times it was possible to purchase cans of beer from our refrigerator. I never liked the taste of beer, so I stuck to Coke. Periodically the army felt generous and sent Sundry Cartons our way. They contained tooth brushes and paste, toilet paper and candy. The candy was invariably one of two types. One was similar to M & M's without the M's on the candy. The other was the notorious "Tropical Bar." Most of them were produced by the Hershey's company and looked like a typical chocolate bar except they were made to withstand high temperatures. They never melted in the hottest temperature; they also did not melt in your mouth. The standard joke was that you could throw them to the Vietnamese children, and they would throw them back at you.

I have never seen marijuana used in Vietnam, but I heard it was quite prevalent in some units. Alcohol was the drug of choice with medics, and for the most part they drank in moderation. There were a few exceptions. On New Year's Eve there was more drinking than normal as would be expected. The infantry battalions were standing down for the holiday, and we were not expecting casualties. I think one of the physicians and

I were the only personnel sober enough to conduct medical business if it should arrive.

Just before midnight we received a radio message that a helicopter was bringing someone with a fever. Sick people needed care; but the most I would need to do was a white blood cell count and malaria smear after the physician evaluated the patient. In the sixties helicopter pilots did not have GPS to guide them. I am not sure how they navigated, but it was not extremely accurate in the dark. Normally when the helicopter was close to the destination, the pilot would request a flare. Someone at the destination would then fire a colored flare. In clear weather the flare was visible two miles away. If the pilot correctly identified the color, he was ushered in. Choosing from a variety of colors prevented the enemy from sending up their own flare to draw the helicopter into an ambush.

When the helicopter was close enough for us to hear its rotor blades, one of the officers fired a colored flare. This should have been uneventful, but this was New Year's Eve, and too many people had over indulged in beer, marijuana, or both. Everyone on perimeter guard had access to flares. The sight of a colorful flare encouraged celebrating soldiers to join the fun. As the helicopter was about to land in the dark, dozens of flares illuminated the night. The bright flares ruined the pilot's night vision. I watched as the helicopter veered from the landing pad and headed for our whip antenna. Our clearing station had its own radio, which used a vertical antenna that protruded at least twenty-five feet into the air. If the chopper blade were to hit the antenna, the helicopter would crash into our clearing station. I wondered who would care for the wounded once the clearing company was obliterated. Fortunately, someone ran to the landing pad with a flashlight to guide the helicopter. All is well that ends well. The physician admitted the patient for observation while I checked his blood for malaria parasites.

We were not forgotten during the holidays, and everyone received care packages filled with candy, cookies, and other treats. Goodies from home filled the barracks tent. Then someone noticed a visitor; it was a rat. He was no doubt visiting from the village that was little more than several hundred yards from our clearing company. The running joke was that the rat preferred American cookies over steamed rice.

The novelty changed to concern when more rats arrived during the coming weeks. I didn't know if they were immigrant rats from the village or the result of rapid breeding. They lived in the pallets that we had placed on our dirt floor. We saw them infrequently when the lights were on, but once the generator was turned off, the barracks tent belonged to them. We could hear them fighting among themselves. We slept on cots that kept us off the ground. For a while that was sufficient, but with time they became bolder and climbed over us searching for food. It seemed there was always one individual getting rabies shots after being bitten in the night.

The rats bothered me more than they bothered the others who took the rats in stride. During my eleven months in Vietnam I had multiple close encounters with death, but nothing instilled fear in me like those rats. I feared going to bed, because the rats owned the night. Each night my fear increased. We had government issued mummy-style sleeping bags. They were too warm for the Vietnam weather, so most people used them for a blanket on the colder nights. For me the sleeping bag was the final defense against the horde of rats. I zipped myself into the sleeping bag until only my face was exposed. Then I rolled over and buried my face in the cot. I was too hot and sweaty to get much sleep. I lay there while the rats crawled over my sleeping bag. Sometimes it was only my imagination, other times I was sure the rats were real. I was rapidly heading toward a mental breakdown.

Then I developed a fever. It was mild at first, and I thought I was merely overheated from the hot sleeping bag. The following day the fever grew worse. I took my temperature; it was 103. A temperature of that magnitude could only mean malaria. I had been taking my antimalarial medicine religiously, but that did not always prevent malaria. I poked my finger and made a Giemsa-stained slide of my blood. It seemed strange searching my own blood for the malarial parasite that I knew was hiding somewhere in my blood. After fifteen minutes I abandoned the search. It was not uncommon to not find the parasite early in the infection. The best time to find the parasite was when the temperature was spiking. About eight hours later my fever spiked again. The second finger poke was also fruitless. On the third day my fever spiked to 103, and I was still without a diagnosis. The physicians decided enough was enough. They ordered my evacuation to the 71st Evac Hospital. As the Med Evac helicopter lifted off the helipad, I waved good-by to the rats of Ban Blech.

The 71st Evac Hospital was technically a mobile hospital but it occupied numerous frame buildings with corrugated metal roofs. I was told they had a 400 bed capacity, but that varied with the needs of war. No patient was ever turned away. The hospital was on the outskirts of Pleiku, not far from the 4th Infantry's base camp, but I had never seen the hospital before. The medivac helicopter circled the landing pad like a cat trying to find a place to lie down. The pilot, apparently satisfied with the direction of the wind, gently lowered his helicopter on top of the white "H."

If I had been a war casualty, a swarm of medical people would have been there to greet me. Since I was merely a patient with a fever, only a lone medic welcomed me. He led me to the medical tent reserved for people with malaria and other non-traumatic medical problems. I was assigned a real bed with real sheets. If I had known that, I would have gotten malaria much sooner. They also had real nurses. It had been months since I had seen a woman.

They did not send me to the 71st Evac Hospital to enjoy the comfort of a plush bed or good conversation with female nurses. They sent me there because I was sick, and I did not disappoint. I think my intake temperature was over 104. The malaria parasites are most prevalent when the fever spikes, so they immediately took blood samples to confirm what everyone knew.

The following morning I was informed that they could not find any parasites. The fevers continued. At one time I think it reached 105. That was the decision point. High fevers can cause brain damage, and any temperature over 105 meant a trip to the dreaded ice water bath. I had yet to experience it, but I talked to many patients who had; it was not a pleasant experience. Since my temperature was not technically over 105, I talked the nurses out of it. They gave me some aspirin and retook my temperature a few minutes later. I could have told them it was not necessary. My fever had broken and I was covered with sweat. This cycle repeated itself over the next several days. Every four hours like clockwork I would develop severe chills. I have never felt so cold. It was like I was already in the ice bath. I could not get warm enough. My fevers would peak over 104 degrees, but I don't think it ever reached 105 again. The nurses took a blood sample every time I had a chill, confident that this time it would reveal the malarial parasite. It never did. When the fever broke, I would be drenched in sweat. The sheets felt like I had wet the bed, except it was mostly under my back. It was difficult to believe I could produce so much sweat. More than once, the nurses had to replace the bedding with dry sheets. The dry sheets felt so good.

After three or four days I counted fifty-two puncture wounds where I had been poked for blood tests of one type or another. Most of them were for malaria smears. I was not getting any better. For the first time in my life I had no desire to eat. Most of the time I ignored the offered food, unless there was a stern nurse supervising my meal. Even then I only nibbled at the meal. I was losing fluid from the fever and sweat, which they replaced with IV fluids. At one point I think I might have been delirious. I remember sitting up and experiencing a strange abdominal sensation that I thought was my empty intestines sloshing around in my abdomen. I thought that was hilarious.

I was evaluated by physicians several times a day. They were all upbeat, but I could tell they were worried. I was dying. It was impossible to continue with the high fevers and chills indefinitely. If I had been injured in combat, they would have notified next of kin. This did not apply to medical illnesses. They assumed the patient was capable of notifying family. I considered it, but there was nothing my family could do.   It would only cause undue worry.

The doctors knew I would die if they did not provide proper treatment, but they still didn't have a diagnosis. They had given up on malaria. It was inconceivable that I could be that sick without one of the dozens of blood smears showing a parasite. One morning a doctor told me he was going to give me some new medicine.

"What medicine is that?" I asked. He held out his hand to show me the pill. In those days we did not worry about touching someone's medication.

"You're a medic. What do you think it is?" he replied.

I looked at the pill and made a wild guess. "Tetracycline?" I asked. He told me I was correct. I later learned it was actually oxytetracycline, but that is close enough for government work. Oxytetracycline is one of the second-generation, broad-spectrum antibiotics belonging to the tetracycline family. Oxytetracycline was a shot in the dark, since they still did have a diagnosis. They sent blood work to Saigon for further study, but that could take weeks.

I was not optimistic that an oral antibiotic would alleviate my symptoms, although if I had an infection, an antibiotic might be helpful. I lay in bed waiting for the next round of chills and fever. They came every four hours. Whatever infection I had was cyclical and punctual. I checked my watch and waited; and waited. The dreaded chills never came. It was hard to believe one small pill could do so much in such a short time. I continued taking the oxytetracycline even after I felt normal. After three days without fever, I was proclaimed cured and sent to the 4th

Infantry's base camp at Camp Enari. Camp Enari can be boring, but at least there were no rats.

After two weeks I was asked to return to the hospital. I bummed a ride on a helicopter heading in that direction. I meet with several physicians from Saigon. They informed me that I had murine typhus. They were all excited. Apparently I was the first American in Vietnam to get the disease. I was flattered. They said that form of typhus is spread by fleas. They asked me if I had been around any animals such as dogs, wild animals, or maybe rats! Rats had been my greatest adversary during my eleven months in Vietnam, but they were also the solution to my pending nervous breakdown.

22

The Tet Offensive

I was again stationed at our basecamp at Camp Enari, just north of Pleiku, and it didn't take long for boredom to set in. I did the unthinkable and volunteered for rent-a-medic duty. I preferred working as a medic, which I found more enjoyable than the general laborer assignments I would otherwise have. I had a friend named Mike Youngdahl who I knew from my Fort Benning days. He was a medic with the 4th Engineering Battalion. When they asked for a medic I jumped at the opportunity thinking I would be working with Mike. That was not to be. He was assigned to a different company.

Working with the engineers was exciting. We got to build bridges. When I say we, I must point out that I was chief supervisor. I sat on a hill overlooking the operation and made mental suggestions. The bridges were temporary pontoon bridges. The engineers transported pontoon sections on large trucks. They launched the pontoons into the river where a bridge was needed. A crew of several engineers lined up the motorized pontoons and then bolted them together. Once completed a 50 ton M60 main battle tank could cross with ease.

On one mission northwest of Pleiku, we were asked to build a bridge over a river, so a tank battalion could cross. We were told we had to construct the bridge, run the tanks across, and then remove the bridge within a three-day time period. Military intelligence said that was how long it would take the enemy to organize an attack. I wondered if military intelligence knew what they were doing.

I found a good spot on a small hill next to the road, which overlooked the river. My assignment consisted of daydreaming while looking alert. That required considerable skill. I had almost dozed off when one of the villagers noticed my aid bag. He pointed to a festering wound. I opened the wound and allowed the pus to drain. Then I applied a dressing with an antibiotic ointment. I wondered if that would be sufficient, but I would not be returning for a follow up visit. It didn't take long for a line to form. Most of my impromptu patients had skin infections, but some were more serious. One older man had a large tumor in his mouth. I am sure it was cancerous. There was nothing I could do. He would have a painful death in his near future. A mother presented a small infant for me to treat. The baby was listless, but breathing. I checked the child's eyes; the pupils were fixed and dilated—a sign of brain death. I had nothing to offer. I still vividly remember those dilated pupils.

That was the last bridge I helped build. We had been hearing rumors of a major offensive by the North Vietnamese, but we were always hearing such rumors. The local Vietnamese were preparing for Tet, which is their New Year. It was the most important celebration in Vietnamese culture and would usher in the year of the monkey. The locals did not appear concerned, and their grapevine was normally more accurate than our military intelligence.

I was sent back to the engineering company, but this time they were not planning to build a bridge. They had .50 caliber machine guns mounted on bulldozers and soldiers walked around with grenades strapped to their belts. This looked serious. The battalion was preparing for a major skirmish, but the officers provided no details—not even rumors. I had been on small recon patrols and larger ambush patrols, but I had never been part of a battalion size military operation.

With no specific orders, the engineers sat on the ground in silence. Everyone was lost in their own thoughts. There was little conversation and then only in whispers. I wondered if people waiting on ships prior to D-day had similar thoughts. Would some of these engineers be dead before the end of the day? Would I be one of them? It was easier when conflict was spontaneous, without warning. Then there is no time to think. Reflexes and training took over.

After two hours we received word that we were being deployed to Pleiku. Pleiku was only a few miles away. We could see smoke from the city rising high into the afternoon sky. The North Vietnamese had taken over the city, and it was up to us to drive them out. It seemed like an ambitious undertaking for one battalion.

I heard helicopters in the distance. Helicopters were not that uncommon, but this sounded like many large chinook helicopters. Chinooks have twin rotors and were capable of hauling large cargo. As they approached, it became clear we were the intended cargo.

They landed in a clearing not far from us, and a Lt. Col. gave the order to load up. I had been quick to volunteer for recon patrols, but their objective was to avoid conflict. Now conflict was our sole purpose. I lingered back with diminished enthusiasm. I was the last one to board the chinook. I had to admit, I was anxious. Hearing inside the Chinook was difficult. An officer at the front was giving directions that I couldn't hear, but word was passed down that we had orders to land in the center of Pleiku and fight our way to the airport on the outskirts of the city. That was an ambitious goal considering the entire city was in flames. The helicopter had few windows. I peered through the closest window. Smoke and fire were everywhere. I couldn't see any hospitable places where we could land. I hoped the pilot had a better view.

The pilot made a couple of circles and then settled down in an open area. The ramp at the back of the helicopter slammed against the ground. Only then did I realize my mistake. I

remembered a Bible verse, "The last shall be first, and the first last." I was the last to climb aboard the Chinook. Now I was facing the exit. Above the roar of the engines I clearly heard an officer yell, "Everyone, out!" I ran from the bowels of the Chinook looking for any place I could hide. As I was making my exit, someone pushed me aside. Obviously, the individual was in a hurry. Once he was fifteen feet from the aircraft, he turned around and snapped a picture; he was a reporter for the *Ivy Leaf*, which was the 4th Division newspaper. The strap on my helmet was coming loose forcing me to hold my helmet. I am afraid I did not appear very ferocious in his photo. The helicopter did not linger long. As soon as the last man's feet hit the ground, the pilot made a strategic retreat; we were on our own.

We all fell to a prone position while our fearless leader decided what to do. I could hear gunfire in the distance. The captain motioned for us to follow him. Of the many directions he could have gone, he decided to head toward the gunfire. We had walked little more than a quarter of a mile when gunfire erupted all about us. I couldn't see anyone actually shooting at us, but the gunfire was unmistakable. Everyone again fell to the ground. I tried to hurdle some razor-barb concertina wire. I was never a track star in high school, and my talent had not improved. One of the razor barbs caught my pants ripping them downward from just below the hip. My leg was mostly bare and the pant leg flapped in the wind. I looked like a seasoned warrior. John Wayne would have been proud.

I fell to the ground behind a small berm along with several others. Some of them were shooting, but I could see no one to shoot at, not that I was looking very hard. At least no one was yelling, "Medic!" What I did see was a large rooster. He climbed to the top of the berm and began to crow. I don't know why I found this irritating. I wasn't sure if the chicken was scared, angry, or just staking out his territory. Either way, he was very arrogant and pompous. I lowered my M-16 and placed him in my sights. At that short distance there was no way I would miss.

I was about to pull the trigger when it occurred to me that the rooster was someone's dinner. I had no right to confiscate what rightfully belonged to someone else even if I found the rooster irritating. I flipped the selector switch back to safety. With all the lead flying through the air, his survival was still in question. About that time I heard what I was hoping I would not hear.

"Where's our medic?" It was the captain. In Vietnam, medics did not wear armbands or red crosses on their helmets. We preferred not to wear targets on our heads. We looked no different than any other soldier. I was hoping some other medic would rise to the challenge—that did not appear to be happening.

"Yes, sir. What do you need?"

"There are some civilians in a bomb shelter about fifty yards in front of the skirmish line."

I looked where he was pointing. There were several houses that had burned to the ground and were still smoldering. Just to the left I saw a thatched bamboo square on the ground. I assumed this was the cover to the bomb shelter. A woman periodically raised her head to see what was happening. That was not a safe place to be, but I wasn't sure where I fit in. They didn't appear injured.

"I need you to escort them to safety back behind our lines." I am sure he could see my concern. "I'll tell everyone you are in front of us."

That was not reassuring. A year earlier two infantrymen got separated from their battalion. Fortunately, they had a radio. As they approached their battalion's perimeter, they called in to let everyone know they were Americans and on the way in. Word was passed down the line, but someone did not receive the information and shot both of them dead. That made headlines when it happened. I did not wish to be a headline. Being killed by friendly fire doesn't even warrant a purple heart. Death by friendly fire happens more often than people appreciate.

I began crawling toward the Vietnamese. I heard no gunfire directed toward me, which was reassuring. A supersonic bullet passing overhead sounds like a stick breaking. Once you hear that sound, you never forget it. Fortunately, no one considered me a target. There was an explosion off to my left. I assumed it was a grenade or a mortar shell. It was too distant to be an immediate concern. I crawled on. I arrived at the bomb shelter the same time as a medic from another company. I had never seen him before. This was irrational, but I felt safer sharing the risk with another person even if he was a total stranger. I now had someone to share any incoming gun fire.

The bomb shelter was nothing more than a large foxhole with a matted roof. The roof offered little protection other than psychological comfort. The hole was large and complex. Too much dirt had been removed for a spur of the moment endeavor. It had to be a multifamily project created over many days. It was a routine project for a nation at war.

An elderly woman climbed out of the shelter. I pushed her to the ground—targets of opportunity attract stray bullets and they could hit me as likely as her. The other medic motioned that he was going into the hole. He was obviously more courageous than I was. If push came to shove, I would have volunteered. I was relieved this was not necessary. He helped another woman climb out of the shelter. I would have guessed she was in her twenties, but with Asians I am a poor judge of age. Several small children followed her out of the bunker. Then my new-found friend passed an infant to me. The baby was cradled in one of the conical hats popular with the Vietnamese people. The baby was that small. The infant smiled at me, oblivious to the surrounding death and destruction. I gave the baby to the woman I assumed was the mother.

"You good, G.I.," she said. I didn't know if she was thanking me or if she was comparing me to other Americans. Not everyone liked us.

We ushered our charges to safety behind our lines. Their home was likely one of the smoldering ruins. They had no place to stay and nothing to eat other than an arrogant rooster. I wondered what became of them, but that was not my problem.

There had been a lot of small arms fire exchanged with soldiers defending a burned out school. This ceased once it was discovered they were ARVN (Army of the Republic of Vietnam) and not North Vietnamese soldiers. With all that gunfire, it was amazing that no one on either side was seriously injured. I did treat one small toddler who had been shot in both legs. It was mostly baby fat and skin, but it would leave a nasty scar.

Dusk was approaching, and it appeared the North Vietnamese army had pulled out of the city. We had achieved our objective, at least in the minds of the higher-ups. We were told to set up a perimeter for the night. There was an advantage to being a medic. No one wished to have their medic killed, so I was allowed to set up housekeeping in the center of our fortification. It was winter time in the northern hemisphere, and it can get chilly in the Central Highlands. I chose a spot next to the burned-out school house. Only the foundation remained, but that was masonry and still retained heat from the fire. I curled up in my poncho liner and pressed my back against the warm wall.

It was a restless night. When I awoke the sky was clear except for patches of smoke. I opened several cans from my C-rations. C-rations normally come in a box and contain a variety of occasionally appetizing foods. It was the custom to remove all the cans from the box. The individual cans are easier to pack in our cargo pants or back pack. The cardboard box also added unneeded weight. I no longer remember what I ate for breakfast. Normal etiquette required that we carry out the empty cans, but at this point, no one seemed to care. I left my garbage next to the burned-out school house.

Rumors are abundant in a combat zone. Some are true and others are false. The current rumor appeared to have some validity. According to the rumor, the invasion of Pleiku was not an isolated event. Someone said there was street fighting in Saigon. I found that difficult to believe, but I was only concerned with the street fighting in Pleiku. I did hope the rumor that the North Vietnamese had pulled out of the Pleiku was true.

I finished my canned breakfast as the engineers—now infantry—were lining up. We still had not reached the airport, which was our original objective. We fanned out in a skirmish line with a sacrificial lamb one hundred yards ahead of us walking point. In theory he would make contact with the enemy before our main body. Risking his life would save many other soldiers. I was glad medics were never assigned to point.

The rumors about the North Vietnamese leaving the city appeared true. We found no sign of enemy resistance. They must have retreated back to the hills during the night, leaving many dead bodies behind. The bodies were contorted with a variety of injuries. Unless they were lying on their backs, I could not distinguish which bodies were ARVN soldiers and which were North Vietnamese. Their uniforms were similar. I found one soldier in a trench. He was on his knees with his head against the ground and his hands holding his abdomen. He must have had a belly wound and probably died a painful death. He was motionless and covered with dust. Dust is easy to come by in the dry season. It was easy to assume he was dead. I debated if I should check for a pulse. That would require climbing into the trench. Often dying soldiers or their comrades pulled the pin on a grenade and covered the arming lever with the dying person's body. Booby traps were a common tactic in the Vietnam War. I told myself he was dead and walked on. I have always regretted that decision.

We reached the air base late in the afternoon. It had been an exhausting two days. With little outside communication, we assumed Pleiku was the center of the offensive. It wasn't until we reached the air force base that we learned the truth. Almost every significant town and city in South Vietnam had been attacked. Even Saigon was overrun, although the North Vietnamese had since been repulsed. No one thought such an organized offensive was possible. It was a very sobering two days. The military tried to put a positive spin on the highly coordinated attacks, but most people were not buying it.

Although I had no wounds, with my torn pants I looked the part of an injured warrior. The reporter from the Ivy Leaf was making the rounds and interviewing people. He could not pass me by. He asked a lot of questions particularly concerning the Vietnamese family. When I look back at what I had done, I did not feel unusually heroic. I gave the interview no further thought.

We spent the night at the air force base and then loaded into trucks the following morning for our trip back to Camp Enari. Pleiku was considered secure, but aggressive fighting continued throughout South Vietnam. Our company's medical resources were thinly spread across the Central Highlands. One small group consisting of a sergeant and four medics was supporting the 1st Battalion, 22nd Inf. north of Kontum. The infantry battalion had flushed the North Vietnamese from the city, but intense fighting continued north of Kontum.

I was considered an excess medic at base camp, and the group north of Kontum needed help. I didn't need to volunteer; my commanding officer did it for me. He was looking for an experienced medic, and unfortunately that was me. He did give me time to change my ripped pants into something more respectable. The road to Kontum was not secure, so I hitched a ride to Kontum on a Bell 47, also known by the army as the H-13 Sioux. The H-13 is a small two-seater helicopter made famous in the M.A.S.H. TV series. It was left over from the Korean War and used mostly for observation. I don't think it was ever used in Vietnam to carry wounded as shown in the TV series. Any stretcher had to be strapped to the outside of the cabin. An opaque cover placed over the stretcher protected the patient from dust and debris. During the Korean War, more than one injured patient awoke in what they thought was a coffin. During the Vietnam War, the larger Huey helicopters evacuated patients. An on-board medic attended to the patient's wounds during the flight.

I strapped myself into the shotgun position and prepared for take-off. The pilot revved up the rotors and gently lifted off the tarmac. Nothing is more exhilarating than flying shotgun on an

H-13. We were encased in a glass bubble that provided three hundred and sixty degrees of visibility. If I looked between my feet I could see the ground disappearing below us.

There are two ways to safely fly a helicopter. Most of the time the helicopters quickly climbed to a thousand feet or more. This was above the range of any ground fire. That had been the extent of my prior helicopter experience. My pilot preferred the second option. As soon as we cleared the radio antennas of base camp, he dropped the helicopter to tree-top level. The theory behind this strategy was that if anyone were to see us from the ground, we would be out of sight before they could react. That was an interesting theory, but I had learned enough from my science courses to know that some theories can't hold water.

Not all cowboys ride horses. We skimmed the tree tops, rising and falling with the terrain. I could see tree leaves on both sides when we dipped into ravines. The H-13 has to be the sports car of the helicopter world. I am not sure if we flew any faster than the bigger helicopters, but the glass bubble magnified the experience.

The pilot landed on an intersection in downtown Kontum. "Someone will pick you up shortly," he said. It would have been more assuring if a limo with chauffeur were waiting on my arrival. There was not a vehicle or soul in sight. I bravely gave the pilot a salute as he lifted off the tarmac.

Someone would surely pick me up, I lied to myself. In the meantime I needed to stay alive. Standing in the middle of the intersection was not wise. I was told the North Vietnamese had been flushed from the city. That was according to military intelligence, which most people viewed as an oxymoron. There could be snipers and other individuals who were separated from their units.

I moved into the shadow of one of the buildings while I assessed my situation. I had two canteens filled with water, which would last a day or two, but I had no food. My unit would provide food once I reached them. I sat down and waited. I looked up and down the street and saw no movement. The merchants had locked their stores and considered it too dangerous to return. If they found the area too dangerous, why was I here? Two hours later I began to question if anyone knew I was stranded in Kontum. It had been a confusing two days. It was possible the medical group I came to join was unaware I was coming. I wasn't a member of the 1st Bat. 22th Inf. Any message concerning my arrival had to go up my chain of command, transfer to the 1st Bat. 22th Inf. and down their chain of command. That was iffy under normal circumstances, and the confusion of the Tet Offensive and its aftermath was not normal. Too many people were transmitting messages over too few radio channels. I hid in the shadows and waited

I gave up all hope of rescue after four hours. I was officially missing in action. No, make that unofficially. No one knew I was missing. The military occasionally "misplaces" personnel. To avoid unnecessary grief, next of kin are not notified until an individual is missing two days. They had yet to begin counting my days.

Medical wisdom has a rule of fours: you can survive four minutes without oxygen, four days without water, and forty days without food. Food was not a major concern, but my two full canteens would not last long. It was time I went into survival mode. I considered an SOS in the center of the intersection. There were always helicopters in the area. Unfortunately, it was difficult to find palm branches or stones to construct a decent SOS.

I decided to explore the area in search of water. All the buildings were locked up, many with iron grates over the entrance. There were no lawns to water and, therefore, no water spigots on the sides of the buildings. I tried not to wander too far from the intersection in case someone did come for me. The chopper pilot dropped me off early in the morning. The sun was now low on the horizon. I ventured farther from my intersection, moving from one shadow to another.

I was six blocks from my intersection when I heard voices in the distance. That could be good or bad, but I was at least no longer alone. I remained in the shadows and listened. I could not make out any words, although they sounded like English. If I judged wrongly, it could mean my death. I remained in the shadows and slowly moved forward. Motion attracts attention. I hoped my slow motion within the shadows would go unnoticed.

The sound was coming from a ring of sandbags in an intersection two blocks from where I stood. Occasionally I could see heads bobbing above the sandbags—Americans! I resisted the urge to rush out to greet them. That could get a person killed. I worked my way into shouting range and announced my presence. They showed neither excitement nor alarm when I entered their perimeter. We wore the same uniform and that was sufficient for them.

There were eight men in all, part of a mortar platoon supporting the 1st of the 22th to our north. Several M-30 4.2 inch mortars sat in the middle of their sandbag perimeter, all of them pointing north. The mortars had a range of about four miles, which confirmed the fighting was not far away. Every few minutes they fired a round. I don't know why, but it was quality entertainment watching the mortar shells slowly get smaller and then vanish into the sky. This was only possible when I focused my eyes parallel to the mortar tube.

It was late in the evening and I had not eaten; I was hungry. My new-found friends had several cases of C-rations and were happy to share. I dug out my p-38 can opener and dug into the canned food. I now had food and two 5-gal cans of water sat next to the cases of C-rations. I also had friends. No one appreciates human companionship until they no longer have it. My biggest fear had been spending several nights alone in a deserted city. I may not have reached my destination, but I was feeling comfortable. I could remain here for several days if needed.

When not firing off a mortar round, my friends read paperback novels or just lay back against the sandbag perimeter and chewed the bull. No one showed any concern for their security. Even with the M-60 machine gun I noticed leaning against the sandbags, it would be difficult fighting off a significant assault. I mentioned my concern to the sergeant in charge, and he informed me they could have helicopter gunships overhead in ten minutes. I didn't know why I hadn't thought of that earlier. If they were coordinating their firepower with the battalion, they had to have radio contact. I asked him to notify my medical group that I needed a ride. He was a bit reluctant as he did not wish to relinquish his personal medic. He made the call and a jeep pulled up two hours later. It had been a long day, but I was no longer missing in action. The sun was setting when we arrived at our medical station. I was home.

With a sergeant and five medics, we were insufficiently equipped to handle combat emergencies. Since the 71st Evac Hospital was only forty-five minutes away, Med-Evac helicopters flew combat injuries directly to the hospital. We worked out of a single GP small tent and treated slivers, minor burns, and fevers. On my second day at our medical outpost, an order came down from the battalion commander. LTC William Junk wanted a medic to pick up a wounded North Vietnamese soldier and deliver him to the 71st Evac Hospital. I didn't know why the regular Med-Evac did not handle the task. According to the Geneva Convention, prisoners of war were to receive the same medical care as our own soldiers.

Since I was the lowest ranking member of our medical group, I was volunteered for the assignment. I grabbed my medical bag and headed toward the landing pad where a Huey helicopter patiently awaited my arrival. Colonel Junk personally provided instructions: I was to deliver the POW alive at the 71st Evac Hospital so military intelligence could interrogate him. I received the impression he was more interested in interrogating the prisoner than saving his life. I would do my best to deliver him alive, because that's what medics do, not because military intelligence wished to interrogate him. I grabbed my aid bag and climbed aboard the helicopter.

I could understand the hatred for the enemy. They hate us and we hate them. That is what war is all about. The pilot informed me that we would be picking up two KIAs. I didn't ask for details, but he provided them anyway. The North Vietnamese captured two American soldiers and decapitated their bodies. It was unclear if the Americans were dead or alive when decapitated. I was relieved when he provided no names. I had friends in the 1st of the 22nd.

"This will be scoop and run," the pilot informed me over the headset. We were coming into a hot LZ and helicopters were prime targets that quickly drew ground fire. The shorter the time on the ground, the safer we would be. We were close to the front line. Within minutes I saw red smoke designating the LZ. The helicopter set down in a clearing with a company of infantry providing perimeter guard.

Two green body bags awaited our arrival. Body bags are rubberized and for the most part air tight once zipped up. Dead bodies are not always fresh, and body fluids would otherwise leak out. Heavy canvas handholds along the sides and at both ends facilitated loading the bags. These body bags were filled with lifeless human remains. Two days ago they were living men with family members awaiting their return home. They were now returning home, but not as their family envisioned. I assumed the severed heads created the large lump over the chests. I stepped aside as several men roughly loaded the dead bodies into the Huey. They were not particularly gentle. It was obvious these were not the first dead bodies they had loaded into a helicopter. War has a way of inuring one's emotions.

Once the body bags were secured in the small cargo bay of the Huey, two men loaded a stretcher with my patient. He could not have been more than fifteen or sixteen. Breathing was shallow, and he was unresponsive other than occasional moaning. Someone had taped a combat-issue dressing to a wound on his bare chest. I was not overly confident about my ability to keep him alive for the forty-five minute flight to the 71st Evac Hospital. I climbed aboard and the helicopter lifted off.

With the two body bags and the stretcher, there was little room to maneuver. I lifted the dressing to view the chest wound. Bubbles of air exuded from the wound with each breath of the patient; he had what is called a sucking chest wound. As the patient tried to inhale, air entered the chest wound instead of the trachea. I opened my aid bag and found a bandage packaged in plastic wrap. I didn't need the bandage. What I needed was an airtight covering for the wound. I cut a large square from the plastic wrap and taped it over the wound on three of the four sides. Now when the patient exhaled, air bubbled out of the open side, but when he inhaled the plastic wrap closed in against the wound, sealing it from the outside. The patient's shallow breathing improved.

I considered giving him morphine for pain, but decided against it. Morphine suppresses respiration. I was here to save his life, not make him comfortable. I assumed his chest cavity was filling with blood. My patient was in hypovolemic shock. He needed fluids if he were to survive. I placed my aid bag under his feet to force what blood still remained in his body toward his head. Then I set about starting an I.V. In the sixties we did not have needles with plastic sheaths. I placed a tourniquet around his arm and looked for a vein—none was promising. I did not worry about cleaning the area with alcohol. He would have more than his share of infections. An infection at the I.V. site was the least of his worries. I was finally able to insert an 18 gauge needle into a vein at the bend of the elbow. I.V. fluids did not come in collapsible plastic bags in the sixties. Fluid would not properly drain from the glass bottle without a vent to allow air to replace the fluid. I inserted a needle into the rubber stopper at the mouth of the bottle. The needle extended into a glass tube that extended the length of the bottle. Bubbles at the end of the glass tube confirmed that fluid was flowing into my patient. If this had been a Med-Evac helicopter there would have been a hook to hang the I.V. bottle. I held the bottle as high as my arm would reach. Both arms were sore when the pilot began his descent toward the 71st Evac Hospital's white H.

Medics quickly took over the care of my patient. My patient was still alive. I had been successful with my share of the patient care. I leaned back to relax.

"You need to move your butt."

I looked at the person addressing me, not understanding his concern until I saw his hand gripping the handle of a body bag. During the whole trip, I had been sitting on a dead body. I should have been shocked, but I wasn't. It was part of my job. What happened to that teenager working for the ambulance company who nearly vomited because a girl had a scalp laceration? It hardly compared to the patient I just delivered to the Evac Hospital. I have frequent thought about that young Vietnamese boy. Did he survive the war? I will never know.

23

Return to Oasis

Following the Tet Offensive the military returned to normal operations, but with dwindling political support in America, the war was never the same. Our clearing company returned to the Oasis. Since this was familiar territory, it did not take long to erect our tents inside the old sandbag walls. I set up my laboratory inside the ward tent. Casualties were few in number, and life was good.

Having fewer casualties did not mean we sat around in lawn chairs sipping piña coladas. With a bit of creative imagination, the military always found tasks for us to perform. Every morning we fell out before breakfast for *police call*. No, we did not call the police. We formed a line and walked through our section of the compound picking up cigarette butts and any other unnatural items that littered the ground. Logic would dictate that doing this once per week would suffice, but the military does not think with logic. Their goal was to ensure everyone was busy. They excelled in this endeavor. Officers were in charge of the police call, but they never bent over to pick up a cigarette butt. If they found such an offending item, they would call an enlisted man to pick it up. I always ran over enthusiastically and firmly placed a foot over the cigarette butt and then asked where it was. It was passive aggressive behavior, but I was good at that.

Other chores that the military had lined up for us were: KP, filling the shower holding tank with water, and daily vehicle maintenance. Every day we had to check the tire pressure and oil levels on all of our vehicles. Each vehicle had a check list of about twenty items. I often feared the vehicles would wear out not from excessive miles, but from the frequent maintenance.

The most hated task was cleaning the two-holer outhouse. For some reason the army would not allow pit toilets. Instead, the waste fell through the hole into a half barrel. With all the people using the outhouse, it did not take long for the barrel to fill up. Every day someone had to pull the two half barrels out from under the outhouse and burn the feces. Feces are not highly flammable and will not burn without help. It required copious amounts of diesel fuel and frequent stirring. The entire process took less than an hour, but it is easy to understand why this was the least desirable assignment.

It took longer to burn if urine was mixed with the feces. To separate the urine, we used a four-inch diameter tube partially buried in the ground for a urinal. Normally, the military prefers vulgar terms, but we also had the NATO phonetic alphabet firmly engrained in our souls. The Pee (or more vulgar term) tube became the Papa Tango. The vulgar term for the outhouse became the Sierra Hotel. It was not uncommon for someone to say, "If you need me, I'll be at the Sierra Hotel."

For some reason, the task never bothered me as much as it did most individuals. Perhaps it was because I frequently packaged stool specimens to be sent to outside labs. What I detested was the multitude of needless tasks assigned each day as well as getting up early for daily formation. I enjoyed my sleep. After conferring with everyone in the unit, I approached the platoon sergeant. I would be willing to do outhouse duty every day if I was given no other assignments. That also included daily formation. The platoon sergeant was tired of all the grumbling when he assigned the task and enthusiastically endorsed my proposal.

Unless we had casualties or work in the lab, I was allowed to sleep as long as I wished. On a good day, I worked no more than an hour. While everyone else was doing frivolous chores, I was lying in bed reading or taking an afternoon nap. Life did not get any better than that.

That all changed a month later when our radio man got promoted to buck sergeant. He decided that I should show up for morning formation. He went through the barracks tent to wake everyone up. I remained on my cot, eyes closed.

"Buege, wake up," he said.

I ignored him. He shoved my shoulder. I remained limp. It became obvious that a major confrontation was in progress. A crowd began to gather. The buck sergeant placed a feather in my ear. I didn't flinch. Every time my adversary found a creative way to torment me, he received applause. Every time I remained composed without flinching, I received applause. He poured water from his canteen on my face. When I continued to feign sleep after he rolled me off the cot, he admitted defeat. He left after stating that he would recommend a court martial. After he left I arose to a standing ovation.

I had considered the consequences to my action. A court martial was one option. The defendant gets to provide his defense with a military-appointed attorney. Enlisted men seldom win such trials. The other option was an article 15 where guilt is admitted and there is usually a reduced penalty It was similar to a plea bargain in civilian law. I was only a private first class, so a reduction in rank did little to lower my current status in the pecking order. With the reduction in rank came a modest reduction in pay. I only had a few months left in the military, so that was insignificant. On the other hand, the military would look silly prosecuting someone for not waking up. It did not take a bored soldier long to decide that the court martial would offer more quality entertainment than the article 15.

The captain in charge of our clearing company was diligently reading the *Ivy Leaf* when the newly promoted buck sergeant presented his complaint. The captain politely listened to the failure-to-awake insubordination while he continued scanning the *Ivy leaf*.

"Buege deserves at least an article 15 for his insubordination," the buck sergeant said as he summed up his accusation.

"Did you know Buege is mentioned in the *Ivy Leaf*," the captain replied. There could not have been better timing. A large photo of several soldiers running from the open door of the Chinook helicopter dominated the front page. The paper did not identify the individuals. In uniform they all looked the same except for one person who was holding on to his helmet. Along with the photograph was a politically-enhanced story about PFC Buege who heroically saved multiple Vietnamese civilians from possible death. No mention was made of the other medic, who was probably more heroic. I was the one the reporter interviewed and that made all the difference. "Tell Buege I want to see him."

Messing with the mind of a newly promoted buck sergeant was acceptable behavior. I was willing to endure the consequences. Ignoring the commanding officer required more resolve than I could muster. I brushed the dust off my boots and headed off to see the captain. I assumed some remorse and groveling was in order.

"You wished to see me, sir?" I said after coming to attention.

"Have you seen the *Ivy Leaf*?" The captain handed me the paper, which I quickly perused. After reading the article, even I was impressed with my heroism. I pointed out that I was the individual holding the helmet. The captain wanted to hear the entire story about how I (with the help of others) drove the North Vietnamese Army out of Pleiku. I tried not to embellish too much and gave credit where credit was due to the other medic. The captain assumed I was just being modest.

"I'm going to recommend you for the Bronze Star," the captain decided after I finished my story. No mention was ever made about my hypersomnia. Two weeks later I was informed that the Bronze Star was denied. I was told it would have been awarded if I had been wounded or if I had been an officer. What I did was considered routine work for a medic and not above and beyond the line of duty. Instead they awarded me with an Army Commendation Medal, which is equivalent to a Boy Scout Merit Badge. I figured the Bronze Star and the court martial canceled each other out. I was happy with that, feeling I did not deserve either one of them. After a couple of weeks the buck sergeant and I were again friends—and I did not have to get up for formation.

Ivy Leaf Feb. 18, 1968   USA Photo by SP4 Larry Eppley

My problems did not stop there. I had been sending rosy letters to my parents telling them I was safe inside my medical lab. I never mentioned my recon patrols or other more dangerous missions. After Tet I told them all the fighting was in Saigon and Hue. Pleiku was a smaller city and didn't get much coverage by the major networks and news media.

Unfortunately, it was covered by our fearless reporter for the *Ivy Leaf*, who happened to be from Michigan. He sent several copies to his parents, who cheerfully forwarded one of the copies to my parents. I had some explaining to do. My next letter explained how the reporter embellished the story and how Tet was a one-time offensive that would not be repeated. I am not sure how much of that they believed, but they were looking for reassurance and my letters provided that reassurance.

Twelve months was the typical Vietnam tour. I have been on tours of the Hershey factory in Pennsylvania and the Gerber factory in Fremont, Michigan. This was not that kind of tour. My first month in Vietnam was petrifying. I assumed bullets would be flying through the air like a summer hailstorm. Most of this misconception was caused by watching too many newscasts prior to my arrival. Yes, people were getting killed, but most Americans returned home without purple hearts. I did not live in constant fear once I established my routine. The last month was also worrisome. I knew the air was no longer saturated with lead, but there still could be a bullet with my name on it.

The army had an early discharge program for individuals returning to college. It wasn't that I just wanted to get out early. I really wanted to return to college. I applied to Grand Rapids Junior College, since I had been there previously. That reduced the paperwork. The college graciously accepted me, and the army granted my thirty-day early discharge request. Now I had to stay alive for another month. That meant no more volunteering for recon patrols or other high-risk assignments.

The thought of a bullet with my name on it was not just paranoia. One individual had five days left in country. He was standing on a pile of sandbags watching a "Fire in the hole." The artillery unit often had unexploded shells in need of disposal. The shells were placed in a hole with a small detonating charge. Just before detonation someone would yell, "Fire in the hole." Watching the explosion from a safe distance was quality entertainment.

The man standing on the sandbags fell before the sound of the explosion reached our ears. He was watching from a safe distance. He should not have been injured, but there was blood on his shirt. He was no longer breathing by the time we reached him. We treated him on the ground where he lay. One of the physicians intubated him, while we inserted two large-bore I.V. needles. We breathed for him using a compression bag filled with oxygen. We gave him several liters of Lactated Ringers I.V. fluid. We followed this with O negative blood. We performed as a well-orchestrated team. Our reaction was perfect, but a piece of shrapnel had clipped the top of his aorta. The blood and I.V. fluid just filled the chest cavity. The physician in charged asked us to stop. As we patted each other on the back for a job well done, a friend of the soldier who had been watching fell to his knees beside his friend and began to cry. Only then did we realize that sometimes, perfect is not good enough. Our patient would be going home, but not to the coming home party he had been expecting.

People who were close to discharge were considered "short." If you said hello to such an individual they frequently replied, "Short." If you were to ask, "How short?" you might receive a reply such as, "I'm so short I would need a stepladder to climb on top of a dime, or I'm so short my feet won't reach the ground, or I'm so short I can walk under a pregnant ant, or I'm so short, I can parachute off a dime and freefall for 10 minutes." We had a long list of "I'm so short" sayings, but sadly I did not write them down and my memory now fails me.

My turn to leave Vietnam finally came. It may seem strange to say this, but a part of me didn't want to leave. Okay, it was only two percent of me. I had made many friends over the prior eleven months. We had been through a lot together. I knew I would never see those friends again, and I would miss them. I wished them well and packed my duffle bag.

I bummed a ride on a med-Evac helicopter to Camp Holloway on the outskirts of Pleiku. Camp Holloway was mostly a helicopter staging area, but they did have a few transport fixed wing planes flying to Cam Ranh Bay. I boarded a twin-engine Air Force transport plane. It was not first class, but we were heading home. About thirty passengers sat on make-shift benches along the walls of the plane with our duffle bags at our feet. I don't think it totally registered that I was leaving until we landed in Cam Rahn Bay.

Cam Rahn Bay is a peninsula that juts out into the Pacific Ocean. It was the most secure real estate in all of Vietnam. No one carried M-16s or wore flack vests. Out processing took twenty-four hours. I filled out many forms and turned in all my equipment except my uniforms. The following day I boarded a commercial airplane with real stewardesses serving complimentary snacks and soft drinks. There was loud cheering as the plane's wheels left the runway and the plane headed east. We were going home.

24

Post-War Years

I knew I would never be the same after eleven months in Vietnam. I slept leaning against a burned-out school during the Tet offensive. I sat on a decapitated corpse while saving the young life of a sworn enemy. I consumed brain tissue from a dying patient. I buried a dead body and other body parts behind our aid station. I felt the loneliness of a silent sky filled with endless stars while the Magic Dragon shattered that silence with thousands of tracer fire. I then relied on the accuracy of unknown artillerymen as their shells exploded around me. How oould I be the same man I was eleven months earlier?

America also changed during my eleven months in Vietnam. It was no longer the land I knew. We were in the middle of the Cold War, and World War II was fresh in our minds. We had seen autocrats like Hitler and Mussolini invade neighboring countries and then impose tyrannical and oppressive laws on the concurred people. Hitler and Mussolini were gone, but now we had Joseph Stalin and later Nikita Khrushchev. When communist North Vietnam invaded South Vietnam, it only seemed logical that we would come to their aid. It began with a few advisors late in the Eisenhower presidency and increased during the Kennedy years.

On August 2, 1964, President Lyndon Johnson claimed North Vietnamese forces had attacked American destroyers in the Gulf of Tonkin. Historians now question the validity of that accusation. Congress passed a resolution almost unanimously allowing the federal government to "take all necessary measures" to protect U.S. forces in Vietnam. The Vietnam conflict was now our war. By 1969 over a half million soldiers were stationed in the war zone. The average tour of duty was twelve months. That required a large pool of replacements. Almost every non-married male would be drafted.

To complicate matters, corruption among the top leadership in the South Vietnamese government was rampant. A military coup attempt in 1960 failed, but in 1963 the president was assassinated and replaced by an equally corrupt military junta. We were no longer supporting the same government we had at the outset.

In hindsight, it is difficult to determine if the resistance to the war was on personal or philosophical grounds, but the movement gathered most of its support from draft age men and their girlfriends who had a stake in the outcome. Those who supported the war were mostly hardhats and older blue-collar workers.

I returned to Grand Rapids Junior College. There were not many colleges willing to accept a student with a GPA of 1.67. Grand Rapids J.C. didn't have dorms. All students commuted to classes, and half of the students were older, non-traditional students. This offered little opportunity for social interaction, and Vietnam didn't provoke the same outrage it did on larger campuses. That provided time for me to acclimatize to the new world order.

The first thing I noticed was people walking about carefree without fear or anxiety. Vietnam was too far away to take seriously. And there were women! The only women I had seen in the prior eleven months had black, shiny teeth, assuming they had any teeth at all. Black teeth were considered a virtue by Vietnamese. The current wisdom at the time was that chewing betel nut created the black teeth, but a special dye may also have been responsible.

The greatest change I saw in myself was that I was now a serious student. I signed up for the most difficult classes. I had second year calculus, calculus-based physics, and organic chemistry, the organic chemistry I had previously flunked. To my surprise I received mostly A's with an occasional B. I had the same I.Q. with an attitude adjustment.

Organic chemistry came with eight hours of lab, where we worked with highly volatile chemicals. Experiments that required dangerous chemicals were performed inside ventilated hoods with sliding glass doors that we could pull down from above when active intervention in the experiment was not required. A six-inch diameter sprinkler hung overhead near the door. Upon viewing it, one would assume it was capable of emitting large quantities of water once activated. A pull-chain hung from the sprinkler. The six-inch diameter ring attached to the end of the chain made for easy activation, should the sprinkler be needed. The architect did not install a drain beneath the shower head, since no one expected it would be needed. All in all, it was a safe laboratory.

It was the middle of the second semester, and I was at my ventilated hood at the far end of the lab. I no longer remember the chemicals we were working with, but they were volatile and highly flammable. We were taking the normal precautions. We had our vents turned on, which sucked all fumes inward. We only lifted our glass shields when we needed to adjust the Bunsen burner or add chemicals.

I was deeply involved in my own experiment when I heard the scream. A student near the door was engulfed in flames. He had lifted the glass on his ventilated hood to make an adjustment. In the process, his beaker must have exploded. The contents ignited by the flame from his Bunsen burner exploded outward, covering the student with burning material as deadly as gasoline.

Everyone in the laboratory froze like rabbits as they watched him dance around, his head and shoulders engulfed with flames. I shoved two people to the ground and plowed through several others before I reached the student. I pushed him under the shower head and pulled on the large ring. A humongous stream of water poured down on him. It was over in seconds, but his hair was singed and he smelled like burned flesh. It was a smell I had experienced before. Blisters covered his face, but I saw no evidence of third degree burns that would be permanently disfiguring. Best of all, he had not inhaled the superheated gas. That would have fried his lungs, and he would have drowned in his own juices.

If it had been two years earlier, I would have frozen like a rabbit along with the others; just as I did on my first ambulance run. Vietnam had taught me many things; one of them was that freezing like a rabbit is not a viable survival skill. That ability to think logically during a crisis would be invaluable years later when I worked in the ER.

There were other invisible changes. I was obsessed with the eleven months I spent in Vietnam. Not a day would pass that some event did not trigger a memory. The memories were not painful or depressing. My best description would be sobering. Any time I cut my lip or tasted blood my thoughts would return to the door gunner whose brain tissue I had imbibed. Gross as that may seem, I felt no emotion other than the fact that the door gunner was one of the patients I could not save. Intellectually, I knew his head wound was too severe for survival.

I was a great fan of the MASH TV show. I loved their mixture of seriousness and gallows humor, although the opening scene with the helicopters bringing patients from over the mountains always produced a moment of sadness. I found the opening theme song particularly depressing. They never sang the lyrics, but I had seen the movie. My mind filled in the words. "Suicide is painless. It brings on many changes."

I don't think of myself as being highly emotional or extremely patriotic, but for the first year after my return, my eyes would water whenever they played the National Anthem. It was a reminder that I was now home.

Another emotion I experienced was survivor's guilt. I have talked with other veterans who shared this experience. I spent eleven months in Vietnam, and I had nothing tangible to document my sacrifice. I was not looking for medals, but a Purple Heart would have been nice. I even fantasized about losing a leg. I wanted it to be a below the knee amputation; I did not want too big of a sacrifice, just enough to prove my worth. In 1967 Bobby Vinton had a hit single with the lyrics; *I am a soldier, a coming home soldier. No purple heart do I wear on my chest. I'm just a soldier, A coming home soldier I know that I, I've done my best.* It was if Bobby Vinton had written the song for me and other veterans, telling us it was OK.

Not all symptoms were emotional. I purchased a Ford Mustang on returning home and commuted to college from Sparta. Almost every afternoon like clockwork I would develop abdominal cramps and spend an hour in my car doubled over in pain. There was no fever, nausea, diarrhea or blood in the stool. I knew it was nerves messing with my gastrointestinal tract, so I did not seek medical attention. Vietnam veterans suffered in silence.

After a year at Grand Rapids Junior College, I considered transferring to Michigan Tech. With 20/20 hindsight, this would have been my best choice, but I had difficulty transferring credits. Instead, I transferred to Michigan State. Michigan State is the largest university in Michigan with over 40,000 students, half of which were male of draft eligible age. I had transferred into the epicenter of the Vietnam protest movement.

Being new to the area, a dormitory seemed the best housing option. I could find off-campus housing the following year if I so desired. I was placed in Wilson Hall. The dorm was set up in suites with two to a room. A bathroom separated the two bedrooms. Sometimes they assigned three to a room in the fall, assuming many freshmen would quickly drop out of school. Since I was older, they paired me with Roger Straw. Our suitemate, Steve Brown was a resident assistant (RA), so he had a room to himself, only three people shared our bathroom.

I did not pick my roommate or suitemate, but I could not have chosen finer individuals. They were friendly and easy to live with, but best of all, they formed a buffer to the anti-war activism that was running rampant across the campus. Vietnam veterans were not the most popular individuals. It was not uncommon to be referred to as "baby killers!"

It was not that Roger and Steve did not have strong feelings about the war; they were both active in the anti-war movement—Roger more so than Steve. Roger had lost a close high school classmate to the war. I could empathize with his feelings. I wish I could have told him that I, too, had lost friends in the war. Some of them died in my arms, but Vietnam veterans did not talk about such matters, unless it was with another veteran. Roger and I talked about the war on many occasions. He did most of the talking, and I did most of the listening. I preferred it that way. Not once did I ever feel that Roger or Steve held it against me because of my veteran status.

In 1969-70 people were beginning to notice that Vietnam veterans were having difficulty adjusting to the new world order. If PTSD was an actual diagnosis at that time, I had not heard of it. I was doing better than many veterans. I did not wake up screaming. I did have repetitive dreams. The most stressful were dreams of not having my M-16. I had never fired it in anger, but it was still my security blanket, and it made me feel safe. I did have one particularly bad dream while at Michigan State. In the dream I was lying in bed while two large rats sat on the bed posts at the foot of my bed. Their eyes glowed yellow and reminded me of the animated rats from *Lady and the Tramp*. I was reliving my fear of rats from Ban Blech. I was half asleep and knew they were not real, but if I were to relax and fall deeper into sleep, they would become real. The rats tormented me throughout the night.

For the most part, I had conquered sleep. Many times Roger would return to the room long after I had fallen asleep. He would tiptoe around in the darkness, so as not to awaken me, but the next morning I could describe everything he quietly did in the dark. Even in my sleep I could differentiate between real threats and the benign.

Tensions peaked in May of 1970. President Nixon announced that the United States had extended its campaign into Cambodia. This left many on campus, particularly anti-war protestors, deeply disturbed. A new wave of rallies and demonstrations erupted on campus. Buildings were burned and vandalized. Damage to buildings on campus the night of May 1st ended up costing the university $40,000 to $50,000.

I found these actions particularly confusing. Those opposed to the military were called militants and militants were called pacifists. The air I was trying to breath was filled with hate.

On Saturday, May 2, officials in Kent, Ohio received threats of violence. Rumors proliferated that radical revolutionaries were in Kent to destroy the city and university. Several merchants were informed if they did not display anti-war slogans, their businesses would be torched and burned to the ground. Kent's police chief told the mayor that a reliable informant said the ROTC building and post office were targeted for destruction that night. There were even unconfirmed rumors of caches of arms and plots to spike the local water supply with LSD. There was an atmosphere that anything could happen.

At Kent State University, about 500 students held a demonstration on May 1st on the Commons. Another rally was planned for May 4 to continue protesting the expansion of the Vietnam War into Cambodia. There was widespread anger, and many protesters issued a call to "bring the war home." A group of history students buried a copy of the United States Constitution to symbolize that Nixon had killed it. A sign was nailed to a tree asking, "Why is the ROTC building still standing?"

Trouble exploded in town around midnight, when people left a bar and began throwing beer bottles at police cars and breaking windows in downtown storefronts. In the process they broke a bank window, setting off an alarm. Police were confronted by a mob of about 120 people who lit a bonfire in the street and continued to throw beer bottles at the police. Mayor LeRoy Satrom declared a state of Emergency and asked Governor Jim Rhodes for assistance. The National Guard was mobilized.

The National Guard did not arrive until late in the evening after the demonstration was well underway on the Kent State campus. The ROTC building was torched. Rioters threw rocks and other objects at the firemen trying to extinguish the flame. Some protesters slashed fire hoses. A later FBI report suggested that a significant portion of the arsonists were not Kent State students.

Emotions were high on both sides when Monday arrived. A protest had been planned at noon, and an estimated 2,000 protesters gathered on the University Commons. The National Guard was asked to disperse the crowd. A campus patrolman riding in a National Guard jeep read the dispersal notice, but he was greeted with rocks and other hurled objects.

Guardsmen were called in. They were trained for floods and tornados, not riots. They had no rubber bullets or body shields. They tried tear gas, but the wind blew it in the wrong direction. There is much conjecture as to what happened next and why. Some say more rocks were thrown. What is known for sure is that at least 29 of the 77 guardsmen fired their weapons at the demonstrators. Four Kent State students died and nine others were wounded. The immediate reaction was to condemn anyone with a military background and I was one of them.

In 1991 a miracle occurred. I had been reliving Vietnam on a daily bases. I could not get Vietnam out of my mind. Then Desert Storm occurred. U.S. troops with the help of allies drove Iranian aggressors out of Kuwait. Our troops returned to a heroes' welcome. It was OK to be a veteran. I felt like someone flipped a switch. My daily flashbacks to Vietnam disappeared. I had not been suffering from PTSD. I had been suffering from shame.

I have been to the Vietnam Memorial on several occasions and have found the name of Craig Yates who was the brother of a high school classmate. I found the name of Allen Jagielo, the fellow medic with the golden voice. There are about a hundred names I do not recognize, but their ships and mine passed in the darkness in that far away land. One name represents a soldier whose body I sat on as I tried to save the life of his teenage foe. I hope that soldier will find room in his heart to forgive me. Another name belongs to a door gunner whose brain I partially consumed. Perhaps it is best that I don't know his name. There is a soldier who is missing a thigh that I buried in Vietnam. The others are faded memories. I sealed many of them in body bags, others I helped stabilize knowing they would die before they reached the 71st Evac Hospital. The war is over for me. I have moved on with my life, but many Vietnam veterans are still fighting that war. I pray they will someday find closure.

The Upper Peninsula Beckons

I left Michigan State in 1972. I had a bachelor in science and a bachelor in arts, but I was no longer a bachelor. I married Nancy Mickey whom I met at the Wesley Foundation at MSU. I had entertained the thought of medical school, but no amount of A's or B's would lift my pre-war GPA of 1.67. My dream of medical school was not to be.

I now had a wife to support, so I fell back on my original goal of becoming a science teacher. That required education classes and student teaching. I could do that more cheaply at Grand Valley State College, so Nancy and I moved to the outskirts of Sparta, Michigan. We rented a small house from a farmer friend I knew. It was small, but there were only two of us and our needs were simple. We paid a total of $65 per month. I was still receiving money from the G.I. Bill. It paid the rent and tuition with a little left over for food. In the fall we supplemented our income by picking apples. We got paid by the number of crates we filled. No matter how fast we worked, we could never keep up with the migrant workers. At the end of the apple season, we had enough money to purchase a vacuum sweeper.

I completed the required education courses during the academic year. All I had left was student teaching, which consisted of one chemistry class. That was not much of a workload for the summer and finances were getting tight. I had worked several years at the local Tastee Treat. The owner was getting older and was not interested in opening it for the summer. After a bit of negotiations, Nancy and I were the managers for the summer.

The most difficult part was investing five hundred dollars to purchase inventory to start the business. My father managed the business before me, and I had worked there for many years. I had done the math. I knew what income the Tastee Treat could create in a summer. My wife was not so sure, but it turned out to be the perfect summer job. Teaching one class of chemistry in the morning was not that time consuming. I was normally back by noon, in time to open the store.

Nancy was in the early stages of a planned pregnancy. According to our plan, she would deliver several months after I started teaching. By then I would have a real salary. What was not planned was her morning sickness. She was to be a dependable employee at the Tastee Treat, but as soon as she opened the door to the Tastee Treat and smelled the bananas, she made an about face. She was of little help until the end of the summer.

Fortunately, we had other good employees. My mathematical projections proved accurate and when we closed shop in the fall, we had converted our five hundred dollars of inventory into a sizeable nest egg. We would need the money when we headed north to the Upper Peninsula.

I accepted a job teaching chemistry and physics at West Iron County High School in Iron River with a starting date of early September. We packed our Mustang and headed north. Once we crossed the Bridge, I assumed we were almost there until I looked at the map; we were only half way there.

With no place to go we pulled into Bewabic State Park, which was half way between Iron River and Crystal Falls. We set up our deluxe pup tent next to a picnic table. It wasn't much, but it was home, sweet home until we could find a place to rent. That couldn't take long, could it? The days turned into weeks. School began and my record of residence was still Bewabic

State Park. We were sleeping on air mattresses and cooking our meals on a camp stove—not the best conditions for a woman in the advanced stages of pregnancy.

There were no secrets in a small town like Iron River. Our plight was well known, and we soon had a lead on a summer home on Chicagon Lake. Rent was now $90 per month, but we had a two-bedroom cabin overlooking a lake. It came with a fireplace and a large pile of wood from a recently cut tree. It only needed splitting, which I did after school. One day upon returning home, I was confronted by irate neighbors who were claiming I was physically abusing my wife. Apparently, my wife who was now obviously pregnant had been splitting wood. That was not acceptable behavior in the U.P. I am not sure if she stopped splitting wood, but she was more discreet when she did.

School was different in the 70s. I had never heard of a teacher's aide. The school expected me to teach chemistry and physics without additional support. I expected nothing less. We had no copy machines. If I needed copies of a test, the office secretary would mimeograph them off if given a two-day notice.

West Iron County was a tough school district. I was constantly disarming students. I told the students if they wanted their guns back, their parents would have to request them during parent-teacher conferences. I never had any takers. At the end of the year, I placed the pistols (fully loaded) on a table where students could retrieve their guns. I reserved two guns for my own self-defense. As they came up to claim their guns, I made sure each student was thoroughly squirted with water. Teaching can be tough.

During the winter of my second year something happened that would drastically change my life—I developed a kidney stone. This was not my first rodeo with kidney stones. They can be very painful. I ended up in the Crystal Falls Hospital for fluids and IV pain control. While I was there, I met a young man in a white coat. He had an otoscope in his pocket and a stethoscope wrapped around his neck. I assumed he was a physician, but he introduced himself as a physician assistant student. What the heck is a physician assistant, I had to ask? He explained it was like hamburger helper. Physician assistants in theory would make physicians more productive. He was in the first class at Western Michigan University. Admission requirements were two years of college and at least a year of medical experience. I more than met both requirements. After several weeks of research, I decided to apply for admission in Michigan's third physician assistant class. I was told the program was very competitive, so I was not optimistic about my chances of acceptance. In the meantime I had classes in physics and chemistry to teach.

Students who sign up for physics or chemistry are often the best the school has to offer. They know where they are going in life, and most of them are college bound. That makes teaching easy, but I did have one student who was different. He was not dumb, but he seemed to have no goal in life. He only did enough to get by. He had friends although I don't know if they were close friends. He was on the quiet side. No one bullied him. He was over six foot, which discouraged potential bullies. I talked to him one on one several times and got nowhere. He was just different.

Then one morning I came to school and discovered he had blown his brains out. In 20-20 hindsight, no one had seen it coming. He gave no warning. There were no overt signs of depression. Students and faculty were shocked. We had lost one of our own and no one knew why. The city fathers and school administrators organized a committee to investigate the suicide and recommend changes that hopefully would prevent future suicides. After consultations with experts in the field, the committee recommended an emergency phone line where distraught individuals could anonymously seek help for their emotional stress. This recommendation was well received by the Iron River community, but what was shocking was their recommendation that student and faculty volunteers staff the phone. We had no experience in crisis counseling. We had failed one individual. Why would we be any better at crisis management now?

Our fears were quickly addressed. The city council and school board brought in experts who provided a two-week training session. After a week of empathy training we advanced to answering phones. The trainers role-played depressed or hysterical individuals. We responded the best we could while the other volunteers eavesdropped. Each scenario was followed by discussion. After the two weeks of training, we felt more confident, but still nervous. Role-playing can never replace the real thing.

I was apprehensive when it came my time to monitor a real phone. Actually, we had two phones; the second phone was available to call for additional support if needed. We had a list of "experts" we could call if it came to that. Iron River provided a small room in their city hall building. It wasn't much, but it was all we needed to answer a phone.

My first shift was boring. I received no phone calls. On the brighter side, that meant no one was contemplating suicide. If they were, they did not wish to discuss their plans with me. I was still a teacher with tests to grade and lessons to prepare. I used the quiet time like a study hall, but I wondered if our project would be worth our effort. We called our project C.A.L. (pronounced call) I am sure it was an acronym; for what, I no longer remember. It received extensive publicity within the community. People knew we were here, but would anyone use it? I only worked one shift a week; it was not that much of a sacrifice.

The third week I settled in and prepared to correct papers. I checked our log book, which was required at the beginning of each shift. No one was receiving calls other than the occasional wrong number. I had corrected no more than a third of my papers when the phone rang. It rang twice before I had the courage to answer. I had visions of someone with a pistol pointing at his head. I don't know why I assumed it was a guy.

I picked up the receiver and introduced myself as John. We all used fake names. To my relief, it was a calm teenage girl with no hint of a pistol to her temple. I gave out a sigh of relief. She didn't even want to talk to me. She asked if there was a woman working the C.A.L. center. I informed her that I was working alone. I checked our schedule and told her when the next woman would be working. It would be several days. She thanked me. I asked if there was any way I could help. She said, "No," and hung up. I entered her call in our log book. We never entered anything other than the beginning and ending of our calls. I didn't save the world, but at least I had a phone call. That was more that most of the volunteers could say.

I returned to grading my papers, but ten minutes later the phone again rang. I was beginning to wonder if there was a full moon. I answered on the first ring with the confidence of a veteran crisis manager. After all, this was my second call. It was the same girl who had called earlier.

"I have to talk to someone now," she said. "I can't wait two days. My girlfriend suggested I call here."

"I will do whatever I can to help," I replied. My confidence following the first call began to wane. It quickly became clear in my mind that I didn't know what I was doing.

"I'm pregnant and can't tell my mother," she said. "I don't know what to do."

A pregnant teenager did not match any scenario we had studied. My training was toward someone with a pistol at the temple. We talked for over an hour. She mostly talked and I mostly listened. Until now, only her boyfriend and her closest girlfriend knew she was pregnant. She assumed her mother would be devastated by the news. In a few months her body would tell everyone she was pregnant. She needed to inform her mother before then.

I suggested she practice telling her mother. I would play the role of her mother. This did not work as intended as we were both consumed by laughter, but we needed the laughter. I offered some medical advice, which was limited to soda crackers for morning sickness. Before we hung up I asked her to let me know how everything worked out. By this time I truly cared about her.

I thought about her many times during the week. I didn't know her name nor did she know mine. I knew she was a senior at our high school. I probably walked past her many times during the week. I assumed it was an unfinished story, and that I would never know the ending. I didn't solve her problem, but perhaps I brightened her day. If I did, I accomplished my job.

The following Saturday, I settled into the C.A.L. Center assuming it would be another quiet evening. The previous week had been a fluke. No one was calling into the Center, but I had hardly started working on my lesson plans for the following week when the phone rang. Why me, I wondered. I answered with what I hoped was a cheerful voice—it was the same teenage girl from the previous week. She had called the Center earlier in the week to see when "John" would be volunteering.

She still hadn't told her mother. Her mother had high expectations for her and that included college. Having a baby did not fall into that scenario. She did not mention it, but I got the impression her mother was a highly-educated single parent. What if her mother disowned her, she wondered. I told her good mothers did not disown their children. We talked for over two hours, sometimes about the pregnancy and sometimes about frivolous matters. Again, she did most of the talking and I did most of the listening. We talked about her boyfriend (very supportive). He was in an awkward position. He couldn't tell his parents until she told her mother. Before I hung up, I gave her my schedule at the C.A.L. in case she again needed someone to talk to.

Over the coming days and weeks, she would call me. I no longer planned on using the time to correct papers or make lesson plans. After my arrival I would sit and watch the phone. Within five or ten minutes, the phone would ring and I knew it would be her. We talked for hours. No subject was off limits. I did not know her name and I didn't think she knew my name.

That made her conversations safe. All conversations eventually returned to her pregnancy. A woman cannot hide a pregnancy forever. Sooner or later the world would know. It was better if she told her mother before that happened.

The school year was coming to a close, and I would soon leave for Kalamazoo where I would enroll in the physician assistant program at Western Michigan University. This may have been selfish on my part, but I wanted closure. I wanted a happy ending. I did not want to leave before my friend resolved her problem.

I knew it was coming to an end during one of my last phone conversations. She had two brothers who were home from college. She found it easier to talk to them about her pregnancy. They did not immediately respond. Then, later they asked her to go for a ride. They drove around Iron River while they discussed her situation. They offered full support. The wagons were slowly beginning to circle around my pregnant friend. That was good, but it also made it more difficult to hide the pregnancy from her mother. Her brothers would not allow that. I knew she would have to tell her mother before our next conversation. With time running out, that would be our last conversation.

I was apprehensive about my last shift at the C.A.L. Center. Training students and teachers to operate a crisis intervention center was a major experiment. I doubt if we prevented any suicides or helped many emotionally stressed people, but it did help one pregnant teenager and in my opinion, that alone made it worthwhile.

I sat at my desk and waited for the phone to ring. I assumed she had told her mother. Maybe I was no longer needed. If so, that would be a success story, but I wanted to talk to her one last time. I wanted to hear that all was well in the family. I waited five minutes, then ten minutes. Usually, she would have called by now. After about fifteen minutes, the phone rang. I picked up the receiver before the ring had finished.

I could tell she was depressed. She was not her normal, cheerful self. She said she told her mother. Her mother didn't yell at her, and there were no lectures as she had expected. Instead, her mother gave her the silent treatment. She would not allow any discussion of the pregnancy. My friend was approaching advanced pregnancy without medical care or family support. She was on her own. I think we were both depressed when we said our final goodbyes.

Leaving Iron River was difficult. A new adventure awaited me at WMU, but I felt like my work in Iron River was incomplete. My wife and I were a young couple. We had not accumulated many possessions. We loaded everything we owned into a U-Haul trailer. On my last day at our cabin on the lake, I received a phone call from the C.A.L. Center. There was a letter waiting for me at the office. I assumed it was a thank-you card for my service.

The letter was addressed to C.A.L., Iron River City Hall Bldg. in Iron River, Michigan and had no return address. Inside was another sealed letter with instructions on the outside: *Please give this to the man who worked Saturday, June 7 from 12-3. Thank you.* I opened the letter.

***

Hi

I'm just sitting here in the hospital thinking about a lot of things. It gets so boring here. When it's not visiting hours, I go nuts. There was a boy brought in from Iron River. I know him a little from school, but not too well. Maybe I'll take a walk and see him later. He is just a couple rooms away.

Well, the reason I'm writing this note to you is because I probably won't get to talk to you again, and I wanted to let you know something. Everything is working out just great! My mother has finally accepted my situation. That has sure made a difference. I'm going to be getting married soon.

The wedding is going to be in Iron Mountain the end of June, probably the 29th Sunday afternoon at David's grandmother's house. She has a beautiful yard. Hopefully it will be a nice day. I've always wanted to get married outside. My brother is going to play guitar and sing. It's going to be a very small wedding with one bridesmaid and one groomsman. I'm really excited. It has always been my idea of a perfect wedding (My mother is doing all the planning!). Can you believe it?

Well, I really wish our little talks didn't have to end and we could keep in touch. It has really done me a lot of good. But they always say, all good things must end. You have really been a good friend to me. I've been able to talk to you about anything, just silly things, not only being pregnant. It was so nice to just have someone to listen to anything I wanted to say. Well, thanks a lot!

Well, the doctor said he might let me go home on Wednesday. I'm getting so restless. Have a nice summer and good luck in college next fall.

***

My world was now complete. The earth was again spinning on its axis. I had been replaced by my friend's mother, and that is the way life should be. I only wish I had one more phone conversation to tell her how much our conversations meant to me. I still have her letter and often think of her. I want to know how her marriage worked out. Getting married at such a young age can be difficult. Did she have a boy or a girl? For some reason I think it would be a girl. She wrote the letter from a hospital bed. I no longer remember the reason for that. She did not mention why she was hospitalized in her letter as if I already knew.

As I write this in 2021 she would be about 62 and her child about 46. I often fantasize that our paths will once again cross. I don't know her name, but she must have known mine. There were not many high school teachers who were leaving to become physician assistants. Perhaps someday when I am selling books at a craft show, she will show up and introduce herself. I will always facetiously remember her as my pregnant girlfriend. Where ever you are, I wish you well.

The P.A. Years
1975

With the Vietnam War escalating in the mid-1960s, many physicians were needed to care for the sick and wounded. This left a shortage of physicians back home. Innovative thinkers at Duke University wondered if mid-level practitioners could fill this gap. They tapped into the large pool of medics returning from Vietnam and enrolled the first physician assistant students in 1965. Other schools soon followed their lead.

I was enrolled in the third PA class at Western Michigan University's PA program. The program was so new few people (including the students) fully realized what a physician assistant was capable of doing. There were no legal definitions or rules to work with. The minimum requirements for admission were two years of college and one year of medical experience. Admission was so competitive that everyone in our class had at least a bachelor's degree. One classmate had a master's degree, and I had two bachelor's degrees. The vast majority of my classmates were navy corpsman or army medics.

My wife and I along with our one and a half year old daughter moved into married housing. We lived on the remains of my G.I. bill, which I supplemented by delivering pizzas on weekends. The first year was all academic work. We had classes in pharmacology, chemistry, and anatomy with a cadaver lab. Since I had a B.S. in chemistry, they allowed me to opt out of the chemistry class. I took a grad level biochemistry course instead.

The second year consisted of a series of six-week rotations in surgery, internal medicine, pediatrics, and family practice. We were given reading assignments during each rotation. This was more fun than the classwork. We got to assist in real surgeries and evaluate real patients.

I learned more in some rotations than in others. One lesson I learned in my psychiatry rotation is well-engrained in my memory. Psychiatry was an abbreviated two-week rotation at the Kalamazoo Psychiatric Hospital. The hospital has been in existence since 1859 and has seen many changes in the treatment of mentally ill patients over the decades. My rotation required one week in the men's facility and one week with the women. The week with the men was uneventful. They were mentally ill but predictable.

I was unprepared for what happened on the women's unit. There was one woman in her thirties who was a bit on the manic side. I was warned to be cautious around her. I thought I was until one day she was in the day room, which was a large room where residents could interact with each other. She was at the far end of the room. I happened to glance at her from a considerable distance. That was my mistake.

"Buege, quit staring at my boobs," she yelled out. Everyone looked at me. By the end of the week, she was pregnant with my baby and asking the nurses if she really had to marry me. The nurses thought it was hilarious. My take home message was that not all women like her are institutionalized. When it comes to he said/she said, people believe the woman. Whenever I performed a breast exam or pelvic exam, I always had a female nurse as a witness. The nurse was not there to protect the patient; she was there to protect me!

Nancy and I wanted two children. Holly was approaching four years old, and we wanted the second child to be close in age, so they could play together. A birth three or four months after I graduated seemed ideal. Then I would be out of school and working a steady job (At least, that was my hope).

I was in my OB/GYN rotation when Nancy became pregnant. She had severe morning sickness. As a joke, I pointed out in my OB/GYN textbook where women with twins have more severe morning sickness. She was not amused. It was hard to find a permanent physician because I moved with each rotation. I made sure she was taking vitamin pills with iron. She didn't have an ultrasound. In the seventies ultrasound was reserved for high risk pregnancies. She continued to grow. Her weight was off the charts. Nancy tried to lose weight. Her arms and legs became skinnier, but her weight continued to climb. I was beginning to suspect twins.

My final rotation was in family practice at Kalkaska, Michigan. Renting an apartment for six weeks was difficult, so we settled in at a KOA just outside of town. Holly loved it because she could swim in the pool every day. Nancy and I slept in a pup tent and Holly slept in a pop-up camper on loan from my parents. Nancy was about five months pregnant and had some issues with sleeping, but with her size, I think any sleeping arrangement would have been a challenge.

Every night I listened to Nancy's abdomen with my stethoscope. I was pretty sure I could hear two separate heart beats, confirming my suspicion of twins. With a little experience, you can feel the infant's head through the abdominal wall. I wasn't sure if it was my imagination, but I thought I could feel three heads even though I could only hear two heartbeats.

Physician assistants belonged to a new profession with no laws to define their role in medicine. Finding a job was not easy. Fortunately, the prison system was looking for medical help. I had an opportunity to graduate on a Friday and begin working as a PA on Monday at the Marquette Branch Prison in Marquette, Michigan. I had a very pregnant wife and needed a job, so I took it thinking I could look for a better job at my leisure.

After finding a place to live, our highest priority was finding an OB physician for Nancy. She was only six and a half months pregnant, but she looked full term. The nurse who initially examined Nancy told her it was just a large baby, but an ultrasound was still ordered. It confirmed not twins, but triplets, and we did it the old fashioned way without fertility pills. That was when Nancy's parents fessed up that there were many multiples in the family tree. About three weeks later, the water broke. Ready or not three babies were on the way. Since they did not have three incubators at Marquette General, we chartered a plane and flew to Grand Rapids where they were delivered by C-section. Because of their small size, they stayed in the neonatal ICU for six weeks. They all did fine.

In 1977, Marquette Branch Prison was the only maximum security prison in Michigan. It was considered the Alcatraz of Michigan where only the baddest of the bad were sent. It opened to its first prisoners in 1889. Like many public buildings in that era, it was constructed from local sandstone. When I arrived in 1975 there were six cell blocks labeled B through G. Brooks Center replaced the original A block, which was demolished and replaced by a medical center and hospital with a surgical suite. That was where I worked. A tall stone wall completed the enclosure. Marquette Branch Prison was an old and intimidating structure that gave the appearance of a medieval castle.

Marquette Branch Prison

I had known many people who have received speeding tickets (including yours truly) and an occasional person arrested for driving under the influence. That had been my exposure to the criminal element. When I began working at MBP, the health records included the patient's criminal record. I found it difficult to believe the normal looking and behaving patient I was examining had killed one or more persons. I think the record that bothered me the most belonged to an individual convicted of "Torture of Child."

Some inmates were more notorious that others. Between July 1967 and July 1969 seven sexual murders were committed with sadistic fury in the Ypsilanti area of Michigan. John Norman

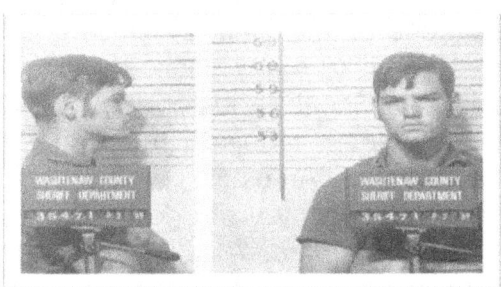

Collins (inmate #126833) was implicated in many of the murders but only convicted of one. Once he was arrested, the serial killings ceased. I got to meet him many times. He seemed like an affable individual with nothing to suggest he was a serial killer. He was not happy with prison life and tried to escape several times. In one clever scheme, he changed his last name to Chapman. This was the name of his biological father, who was a Canadian citizen. He then applied for an exchange with an American inmate in Canada. In Canada he would be eligible for parole. Everyone knew John Norman Collins, but no one knew John Norman Chapman. The paperwork would have gone through if an inmate had not alerted authorities. More information about the Ypsilanti mass murders can be found in the book *The Michigan Murders* by Edward Keyes if you can find it in a library or used bookstore.

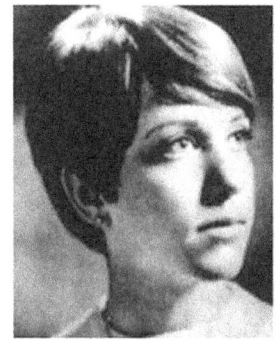

Karen Sue Beineman

The Seven Victims.

Mary Fleszar

Joan Schell

Roxie Phillips

Maralynn Skelton

Dawn Basom

Alice Kalom

Another infamous murderer was John Carl Fry. He was a pimp for Dawn Spens. Together they killed and dismembered a well-known Grosse Pointe psychologist by the name of Dr. Alan Canty. They scattered his body parts up and down I-75. The background story is well documented in *Masquerade* by Lowell Cauffiel.

With so many hardened criminals, many employees felt intimidated. We had more than one male nurse quit after one day, while petite female nurses adjusted well. I had respect for the inherent dangers that went with the job, but I did not live in fear. The Department of Corrections did give us two weeks of Aikido training. I only used my Aikido training once.

B block housed some of the worst inmates. Inmates from the other cell blocks came to Brooks Center for medical care. Except for severe emergencies, I examined B block patients in a small room attached to B block. The room was empty except for my medical bag and a metal chair in the center of the room where the inmate sat while being examined. Most patients are cooperative and appreciative, but sometimes we have to tell them no, especially when they are seeking drugs. I had one patient who was extremely unhappy. He stood up and raised his chair to swing it at me. That was when my Aikido training kicked in. The normal reaction to a man about to swing a chair at you is to raise your arms and step back. Aikido teaches the opposite. Instead of backing up, I leaned forward and grabbed the chair before it had acquired any momentum. It is all the Aikido I remembered. Fortunately, two guards decided the patient was no longer sick and hauled him back to his cell. The chair is now bolted to the concrete floor by a sturdy chain—all in my honor.

The easiest way to break out of prison is to feign an illness that requires transfer to an outside hospital. To reduce this risk, the prison provided most services in house. We had a ten-bed hospital, a surgical suite for minor surgeries, a laboratory, and an X-ray department. When the X-ray tech resigned, I was given the additional responsibility of taking X-rays. This was back in the days of film. It gave me the opportunity to see many unusual X-rays.

We had one elderly black gentleman sent in from a prison farm. Guards were finding nuts and bolts in the toilet and suspected he was eating them. An abdominal X-ray revealed nuts, bolts, stones and bent nails. It was easy to assume he was mentally ill, but we found no evidence of mental illness after an extensive evaluation. He grew up in the segregate south where healthcare was nonexistent. He probably treated ailments with folklore. Perhaps he thought swallowing metal and stones provided iron and other nutrients.

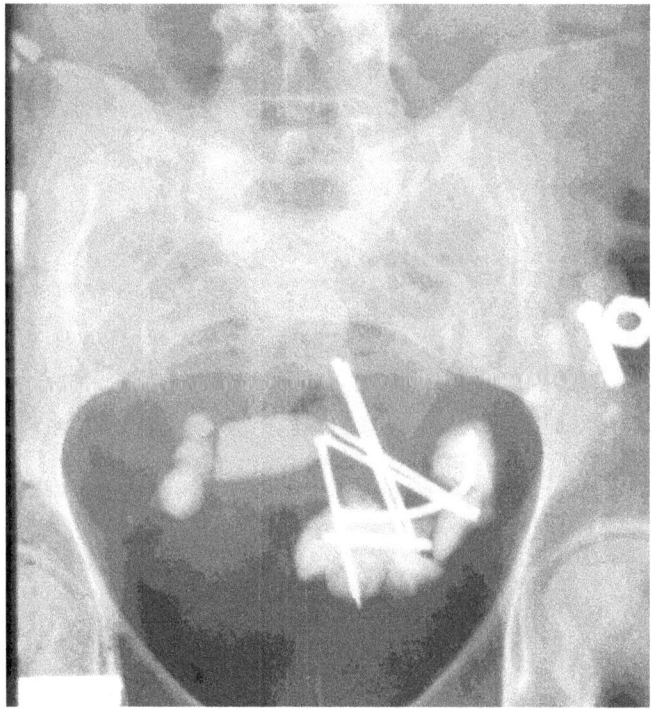

Large intestine filled with nuts, bolts, bent nails, and stones.

The ascending colon on the right side is filled with watery stool. Gravity kept pulling the heavy stones and metal down.

The only way to evacuate the stones and metal was to keep the patient flat in bed. He passed the objects normally.

Sometimes I took X-rays for security and not medical reasons. Many items are considered contraband. That does not mean inmates do not have them hidden away. One inmate was notorious for hiding contraband in his rectum. He would show officers the contraband, but by the time they opened the cell to retrieve the unauthorized item, it was gone. A pelvic X-ray confirmed the hiding spot.

Cavity searches are common locker-room talk and on some media outlets, but in reality a cavity search is not possible on an unwilling patient. The best we could do was lock the inmate naked in solitary confinement and wait.

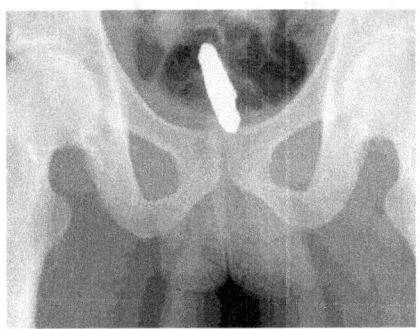

Pocket Knife

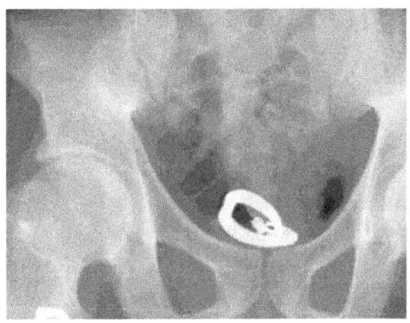

Lady's Watch

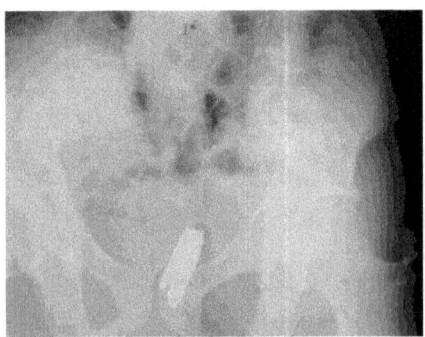

Nail Clipper

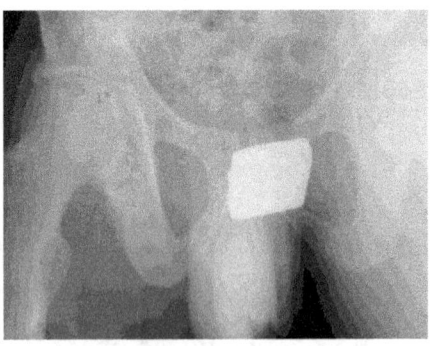

Cigarette Lighter

Sometimes I did not even X-ray people. That is when prison work becomes interesting. Every inmate had a weapon on his person or in an easily retrievable location. Officers considered it good sport to say to an inmate as he passed by, "Hey, you dropped your knife." The inmate would look around with acute anxiety.

Some of the homemade weapons were ingenious. My favorites were the toilet paper guns. If given enough time and enough damp toilet paper inmates can braid a rope that will bear the weight of an adult. They can also fashion a gun. Inmates used old battery casings for the gun barrel. Match heads were used for gunpowder and small stones, nuts, or screws for the "shot." This was held together by molded toilet paper. There were two methods for firing the gun: Sometimes a hole was left at the base of the barrel and the gun was fired like a cannon. A more sophisticated method uses a paper clip wrapped around a match head. A striker plate is embedded in the toilet paper. When the paper clip is pulled, it ignites the powder. This does not always work, but one gun shot a projectile the length of a cell block and made a hole in a window.

The above X-ray is looking down on the toilet paper pistol. The exposure was set to show the inside of the gun; therefore, the toilet paper is not visible. The right half of the battery casing is filled with match heads. The small hole use to ignite the weapon is visible. Thumbtacks and stones provide the projectile.

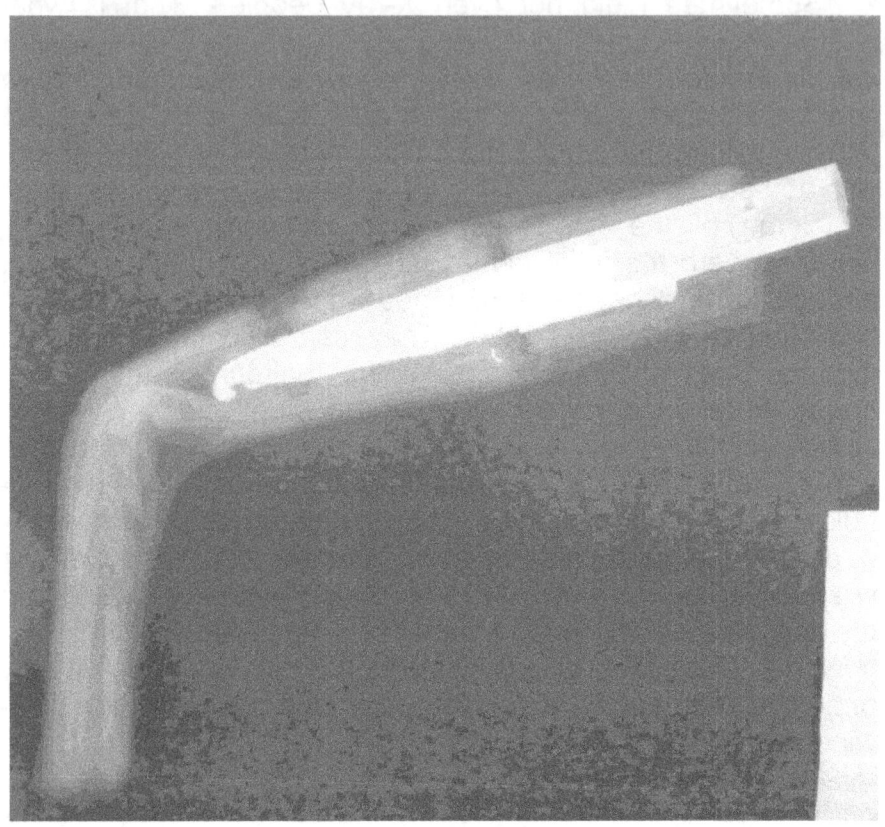

The above X-ray was taken at a lower exposure. It provides more detail of the toilet paper frame. You may wonder how inmates come up with such ingenious devices—they have plenty of time on their hands.

For the most part, my fifteen years at Marquette Branch Prison were boring. That changed in the spring of 1981. In the middle of May, inmates boycotted breakfast to protest the reduced milk rations. The cows at the prison farm were not producing as much milk as usual and the inmates were not happy. Tension declined but persisted. During the last week in May the downstate Jackson Prison experienced two uprisings in a five day period. The Ionia Prison staged a sympathy riot. The stage was set for a riot at Marquette Branch Prison.

On May 26th Marquette Branch Prison saw its first full-scale riot in its 92 year history. When the "Yard" period ended, about 200 inmates refused to return to their cells. The inmates surrounded the guards. There were about 400 inmates in the yard at that time. Any inmate returning to a cell block was booed and jeered. Peer pressure is a mighty force. Officers in the guard towers fired into the ground, but the mob was not deterred.

Off-duty employees were summoned back to the prison. When I arrived smoke was billowing up from at least three of the interior buildings. No attempt to reclaim the prison was possible until all the employees were accounted for. A hostage situation changes the response options.

Officer David Kirkwood was missing. He was trapped in G Block which is the farthest block from the central control building. He remained to allow inmates who did not wish to be involved in the riot to return to their cells. The officer in the guard tower above him provided some security, but the path across the yard to safety was controlled by violent inmates armed with any weapons they could find. Kirkwood had misgivings when six inmates approached him.

"We will get you to safety," they said. "Kirkwood, you have to trust us." When the yard outside of G-Block seemed quiet, the six inmates ushered Kirkwood toward the Rotunda. They were met half way across the yard by officers coming to rescue him.

There were a lot of inmates involved in the riot, but there were many who wanted no part of it and felt the same fear as Officer Kirkwood. Pedro Villalobos was a gentleman in his seventies, and he was a true gentleman. He was from San Antonio. As a teenager he drove to Detroit to visit a friend. He got drunk and killed a man. Fifty years later he was still in prison. To earn spending money, he polished shoes for the guards and also for me. He was humble and well respected. I once asked him what he would do if he got paroled. He said he would get drunk, and then return to the prison to find a place to sleep. I asked him what he did during the riot. He told me he hid and prayed that the riot would soon be over. I asked if he prayed in English or Spanish. Spanish, he replied. It comes faster.

With Kirkwood rescued, the officers could begin reclaiming the prison yard. They have special units trained for such actions. About thirty officers with face shields and pump action shotguns formed a line in front of the rioters. One would think they would have semiautomatic shotguns instead of pump action shotguns, but I am told there is nothing more intimidating than hearing the sound of thirty shotguns locking and loading in unison.

The officer in charge of the riot squad used a bull horn to ask the inmates to return to their cells. The inmates stood their ground. The riot squad was ordered to aim their shotguns five feet in front of the inmates. No one moved. The order to fire was given. Stones and buckshot ricocheted against the rioters' legs. Again the rioters ignored the request to return to their cells. The commander ordered the guards to aim at the chests. This was followed by a stampede back to the cell blocks. The riot was over.

Fortunately, no one died in the riot. Eight officers had injuries requiring treatment. Most of them were contusions and minor lacerations, but there was also a broken jaw and fractured ribs. Fire fighters from the city of Marquette, Marquette Township, Chocolay Township, Negaunee, and the K.I. Sawyer Air Force Base assisted in putting out the fires. Fire still totally destroyed the vocational building. The inmate store, machine shop, and some of the other buildings were severely damaged, but repairable. Total damage was estimated at three million dollars. Readers who wish to learn more about Marquette Branch Prison are urged to read *One Hundred Years at Hard Labor* by Ike Wood. Ike was a prison employee and friend who held many titles at the prison from 1943 until his retirement in 1978.

The vocational building was totally destroyed. This housed academic and on-the-job training classes. Inmates had destroyed a vital resource needed for their success after prison.

The industrial building, aka garment factory, received extensive internal fire damage, but the structure remained solid. After repairs were made, it was placed back in service.

I accepted the job at Marquette Branch Prison with the intention of staying six to twelve months while I searched for a better job. Fifteen years later I was still there. In 1995 there was a severe shortage of physicians and the demand for PAs went through the roof. I had headhunters calling me day and night with offers of generous salaries. I do not live for money, but I had four kids in high school who would soon be thinking of college. Marquette General Hospital made me an offer I couldn't refuse. I would be working in the in-patient psychiatric ward taking care of the medical problems that often arose. Psychiatrists were good at their specialty, but they knew nothing about routine medical problems. It was a salaried position that was supposed to average forty hours a week, but I found myself going to work at eight in the morning and not leaving until eight or ten o'clock at night. After a year of this the psychiatric PAs got together and demanded the hospital hire another PA. Their response was to lay off one of the existing PAs. The remaining PAs immediately began looking for new employment.

I had been offered a job at the Helen Newberry Joy hospital in Newberry, Michigan two weeks after I accepted the job at Marquette General. I might have accepted that job if I hadn't already committed to MGH. I gave HNJH a call, and they were still looking for a second PA to work in their Walk-in Clinic. It required 10 hours per day four days per week. I had four kids in high school. They told me I could take the job, but they were staying in Marquette. HNJH was understanding and willing to provide a room at the hospital.

Helen Newberry Joy Hospital is a very small hospital with an even smaller ER. The ER consisted of one room the size of a two-car garage. There was no ER staff. If a patient arrived in the ER, a nurse and ward clerk from the hospital were reassigned to the ER. There was always a physician on-call, but if the on-call physician was seeing scheduled patients, it became very inconvenient. If it occurred after hours, the on-call physician had to get dressed, shovel snow out of the driveway and drive to the ER.

Bob Barkus who was the other PA and I were asked if we were willing to take first call for all ER patients. It came with a generous financial incentive. We jumped at the chance. As long as I was living at the hospital, I might just as well work.

The ER was a quantum leap above my qualifications. We had physician backup, but in the middle of the night that could be a half hour away. I needed more training. First stop was certification in Advanced Cardiac Life Support (ACLS) at Marquette General. Training included intubation, cardiac rhythm recognition, emergency medications, and defibrillation.

My first chance to use my ACLS came in the middle of the night. I was awakened by a call from the nurses' station. One of their patients was in cardiac arrest. I arrived at the bedside moments later wearing a tee shirt, pants, and one sock. I looked at the monitor: the patient was in obvious ventricular fibrillation. I looked at the patient: he was unresponsive. I hesitated. Then I remembered the well-worn adage that you can't kill a dead man. I set the defibrillator to 200 joules and placed the paddles on the man's bare chest and pushed the buttons. The man twitched and then asked if he could have a cup of coffee. He was unaware that his heart had stopped.

Bob and I also became certified in Advanced Trauma Life Support (ATLS) in which we learned how to insert chest tubes, subclavian IVs, and manage a variety of trauma injuries. My favorite course was a week of wound care taught by plastic surgeons in California. We were given "fresh" cadavers and were allowed to create a variety of wounds to repair.

Most of the doctors at the hospital were family practice physicians who had no interest in the ER. This may be bragging, but I think Bob and I had better ER skills than any physician in the hospital save one.

We once had a backup internist who was napping on the portable delivery table. The nurses chased him off, telling him there was an expectant mother about to give birth in the ER. To this day he denies he was ever told of the impending delivery. It was my first delivery since PA school. Three weeks earlier I had completed certification in Advanced Life Support in Obstetrics (ALSO).

We frequently had visits from drug representatives. Many healthcare providers were reluctant to speak to them. I treated them with the same respect I would any individual. They were only trying to make a living; but, like used car salesmen, I needed to listen with a skeptical ear. Drug companies developed new and useful drugs. As a healthcare provider, I needed this information, but I only believed the data they were willing to submit on paper. By law they couldn't provide false or inaccurate data.

One day I was talking to Amy Buck. I no longer remember what drug she was pushing. The conversation drifted to how I became a physician assistant. I told her I was a medic in Vietnam. She said thank you for your service. Today it is a cliché, but this was the 1990s, and I had never heard that expression. I stared at her in disbelief as I tried to decide if she were mocking me. That would have been out of character for her. There was a very awkward silence. Finally, one of us changed the subject. Looking back, I fear I was incredibly rude. Amy, if you ever read this biography, please accept my apology.

In 2006 I retired at age sixty. I had a wonderful career in medicine that never would have happened if I had better grades and had not been drafted. It also would not have happened if I hadn't had a kidney stone in a hospital that happened to have a visiting PA student. Life is a culmination of random chances.

26

Cancer

Life changed drastically in 1999. I had a persistent cough with laryngitis. After a month I knew it needed evaluation. Cancer was high on my list of probabilities. I made an appointment with Dr. Craig Stien, an ear, nose, and throat doctor I worked with during my prison days. He inserted a fiberoptic scope down my nose to examine my vocal cords and discovered a small nodule on the left side. He assured me that there was nothing to worry about. He was close to retirement and had never seen vocal cord cancer in a non-smoker. Since my smoking history consisted of one cigarette behind the wood shed, I shared his optimism. The most likely diagnosis was a singer's nodule, also known as a screamer's nodule, caused by excessive use of the vocal cords. No matter what it was, it needed to be removed. I couldn't continue with my chronic hoarseness.

Dr. Stien scheduled me for outpatient surgery. It was to be a quick fix, and I would only miss a day or two from work. When I awoke from the surgery, Dr. Stien was no longer optimistic. He was now talking about cancer but wouldn't know until the biopsy report came back. He said he was 90% sure based on the characteristics of the nodule.

Cancer is such an ugly word. I envisioned a painful and miserable death. When I was growing up, my grandmother

warned us we would get death-of-pneumonia if we went outside
in the winter without a hat. She was born before penicillin. To
her death-of-pneumonia was one word. People with pneumonia
died. I grew up thinking cancer was a death sentence even
though I knew people who had survived. It was a sobering
diagnosis.

My fate and treatment depended on the recommendations
of a tumor board consisting of various oncologists. While I was
awaiting their verdict, I sequestered myself in the hospital
library, reviewing the literature on vocal cord cancer. It didn't
look good. Survival might require a total laryngectomy with a
breathing tube in my neck for the rest of my life. Any speech
might require a vibrator held to my throat. I liked to talk and
wondered if I could tolerate that lifestyle.

Fortunately, the tumor board was more optimistic, since the
cancer was isolated. They recommended radiation treatment,
suggesting a 90% cure rate with no damage to the vocal cords. I
could live with that. I assumed radiation would be a piece of
cake.

The radiation oncologist scheduled five treatments per week
for six weeks. Since the radiation beam required perfect aiming,
I was fitted with a fiberglass mesh to enclose my head. Two
holes for my nostrils allowed me to breath. Once I was strapped
into my fiberglass mask, the technicians could accurately aim
the beam during each session.

The first week was uneventful, which confirmed my
suspicion that radiation would be a piece of cake. After the
second week I had a mildly sore throat. I didn't even take aspirin
or Tylenol. The third week felt like I was gargling with hot coals.
I began using Tylenol #3 (with codeine) at night to sleep.

I was too sick to work and it hurt too much to talk. Out of
boredom, I began sending e-mails to close friends to update
them on my condition. I was now in a position where I either had
to cry or laugh. I always preferred the latter. I sent out a
humorous account of my misfortune. My e-mail elicited
numerous responses. It does not take much to encourage me. I

began sending out weekly humorous e-mails. Today, it would be called a blog, but blogs had yet to be invented.

I didn't think it could get any worse after the fourth week, but I still had two weeks to go. I had an appointment with Dr. Stien who looked down my nose with his fiberoptic scope. He described the entire larynx as one huge canker sore. He was impressed; I was not. I began taking Dilaudid (hydromorphone) for pain. It made me sleepy, but I was willing to sleep until my six weeks of radiation were over. It was extremely painful to even swallow. One time I coughed up what had to be a half-cup of pure slime. At times I feared I would drown in my own secretions, but the cheerful weekly e-mails continued. Somehow, I survived the six weeks and began to recover. I was able to return to work cancer free, or so I thought.

After any cancer treatment there is a waiting period. Statistically, I had a 90% chance of being cancer free, but that leaves a 10% chance that not all the cancer was destroyed. The way my throat felt after six weeks of radiation, I didn't think any cancer cells could have survived. Dr. Stien checked my vocal cords after six months and found a suspicious area. A repeat exam at one year revealed a growth on the left vocal cord. We both knew what that meant. A biopsy confirmed the cancer had returned. I was in the 10% where radiation failed. Boy, did I feel special.

It was time for surgery. Dr. Stien said he could do the surgery, but would feel better if the surgery was done at a university hospital. He referred me to Dr. Douglas Chepeha and Dr. Theodoros Teknos at the University of Michigan Hospital. Dr. Chepeha had worked with a physician in Canada who had a technique for removing the vocal cord and attaching fascia to the arytenoid cartilage such that the repaired vocal cord would be movable and functional. The procedure had never been performed at U of M. The entire procedure would take about twelve hours. I knew I would have tough sledding following the surgery. I should have been scared. I should have been anxious, but I was not. That surprised me. I was actually looking forward to getting it over with, so I could get on with life.

I woke up in the recovery room with my family surrounding my bed. They were all smiles. I wondered if they were fake smiles. I was too groggy to care. I am sure the physicians organized the gathering to prove I was still alive. The second time I awoke I was alone in the room. My mind was clearer, and I was able to assess the damage. I had two I.V.s running; one in the foot and one in the arm. I had a urinary catheter in place, so I did not have to worry about peeing. I had three drainage tubes inserted into my scalp and neck to drain any residual blood. These were attached to suction bags that collected the blood. The most annoying and most important medical attachment was the tracheal tube in my neck. This had an inflatable cuff that sealed the trachea and prevented secretions from draining into my lungs from my oral pharynx. This also prevented me from talking or breathing through the nose or mouth. Topping off the list of tubes was a nasal-gastric feeding tube. To prevent the tube from accidentally being pulled out, the surgeons sutured it to my nasal septum. This only hurt when it was accidentally pulled, which was quite frequently.

I lay in bed waiting for depression to set in. I had eleven tubes attached to my body. I could not talk. I could not even roll over. I had every right to be depressed, but the depression never came. There was a TV in the room, but it was hard to turn my neck to watch. Instead, I listened to classical music coming out of a MSU public radio station. With a private room, I could listen to it all night. It felt strange being in a University of Michigan Hospital while listening to a Michigan State radio station. Such is life.

I had resumed my e-mail/blogs and gave credit to the e-mails for keeping me sane. It is difficult to write humorous descriptions of my daily activities and still be depressed. Since I could not talk and had no access to a computer, I wrote my e-mail in long hand and had my oldest daughter post the e-mail. I now had over forty followers.

The tubes came out one by one. I rejoiced with each tube removed. When the body attachments were reduced to the feeding tube and the trachea tube, I was allowed to go home. On July 11th, thirty-seven days after the surgery, I returned to Ann Arbor to have the trach removed. It felt good to talk again. The goal of the surgery was to attach fascia from my temple to the arytenoid cartilage. Then when the arytenoid moved, it would also move the artificial vocal cord. This worked for a while, and I could talk in two separate pitches. Eventually, scar tissue covered the arytenoid, freezing it in place. I could talk, but my voice was very breathy. I continued following up at Ann Arbor every six months until they gave me a five year survival pin. I had survived.

27

An Author is Born

The cancer years were a trying time. Until I received my five-year survival pin, I did not know if I would survive or if I did, would I be able to carry on a conversation. Talking while holding a vibrator to my throat would not be adequate for a physician assistant. With my deep, throaty voice, I was sure I could qualify for welfare. Many people need welfare, but I would accept welfare only as a last resort. I wanted to earn my keep. If I couldn't work as a physician assistant, what could I do? Almost every job required speech—except writing. But I knew nothing about writing. I slept though English classes and didn't know the difference between a phrase and a clause. I also couldn't spell. Any English paper I wrote was downgraded to a C on spelling alone.

On the positive side, I had been sending humorous e-mails that people seemed to enjoy. I had over forty people who asked to be on my e-mail list. Even after the radiation when I was no longer sending e-mails, I had requests for the transcripts. To save time, I posted the e-mails on a web site and forgot about them. If people asked, I referred them to the web site. Then one day I decided to add a counter to the web site. It also collected information about my viewing audience. I was shocked to discover people from forty-four countries had visited my site. Cancer truly knows no borders. The web site is http://larrybuege.com/Updates/update.html, but it may not be available for future readers.

The response I received from my e-mails as well as the spell checker now available on Microsoft Word offered encouragement. Perhaps I could learn to write. I began reading text books on grammar and punctuation. My goal was a full novel, but that was like running a marathon. It was a goal that many people wanted to achieve but few people did.

I decided to secretly write my novel. That way I could save face when I failed. If you failed in a woods and no one was there to document your failure, did you actually fail? I didn't think so. I lived at the hospital four days at a time, and there was often free time between ER patients in the evening. It still took me over two months to write the first chapter.

One evening I had a patient with a possible broken forearm. I sent him to radiology for an X-ray. While I waited, I reviewed my first chapter. It seemed good enough, but I was biased. I had placed a lot of effort into the chapter. It was hard to believe it was anything other than perfect. I set the manuscript aside when the patient returned with the X-ray; the radius was fractured, and the patient needed a cast.

It was late in the evening when I discharged the patient. I headed for my room. I learned that a good night's sleep is not guaranteed. Staying up late is never a good idea. When I awoke the next morning, my manuscript was gone. I tried to remember when I last had it. I rushed to the ER only to find a group of nurses huddled around my manuscript. Their only comment was, "Where's chapter two?"

I had been outed. I was forced out of the closet. There was no way to turn back and still save face. My pride was on the line. Every time I finished a chapter, I would give it to the nurses. It was like throwing bread crumbs at seagulls; it ended in a feeding frenzy. I would be lying if I said it wasn't flattering. I am not sure if I would have finished the novel without their constant encouragement.

It still took over two years to complete *Bear Creek*. When I finished I knew it would be a best seller. I would be on Oprah. I think every writer feels that way about their first novel. I placed the manuscript in a drawer and retrieved it three months later. I could not believe I wrote that garbage. I think I have re-written *Bear Creek* four or five times. As my writing skills improved, so did *Bear Creek*. It is still my favorite novel.

As I mentioned in the previous chapter, I survived to the five-year mark and was able to return to my old job with no fear of the cancer returning. I no longer needed to write as an occupation, but I was hooked. I enjoyed writing. This autobiography will be my tenth book. At first I tried to have my novels traditionally published. That required submitting numerous query letters to agents, who would then pitch the manuscript to the big five publishers. I burned through two agents. They were both minor league. One had mental problems and just disappeared. The other agent decided he would rather be a drummer in a rock band.

Writing books is no fun unless someone reads them. I decided to self-publish my novels. There are advantages to self-publishing: you are your own boss and the profit margin is much greater than with traditional publishing. I sold the novels at craft shows and discovered I also enjoyed talking to readers even though I did not have much of a voice.

In addition to my novels, I have authored numerous short stories. *Frozen Memories* received first place honors in a regional short story contest and *Troubled Waters* took third place in an international writing contest. The *Song of Minnehaha* was published in the first *U.P. Reader* as well as the *Huffington Post*, which is a national newspaper. My only regret with my writing career is that my novels and short stories will die with me. For this I apologize to my great, great, grandsons and granddaughters. I wish you could have read some of my works. I am hoping you will discover this autobiography in someone's attic and think I lived an interesting life.

28

And then I Died

I like to think I am a good writer, but writing my own obituary was a challenge. One would think that a physician assistant could at least document the cause of death, but this remains unclear. I have numerous thyroid nodules that could turn to cancer at any moment. Cancer is not a good way to die. I am now seventy-five, and I am sure my heart is past its warranty. Ventricular fibrillation in the middle of the night would not be a bad way to go. Then there is that chronic progressive disease that I have had for over twenty years. Even Mayo Clinic cannot validate it with a label. I have named it after the physician assistant who discovered me. She is a modest person, so I will not mention her here. Let's just agree that I died.

At my funeral, people will gather around my casket or more likely a pile of ashes, since it is becoming difficult to find real estate in which to hide the bodies. There will be an American flag neatly folded in a triangle, assuming the veteran organizations are still providing flags to veterans. Someone will look at my pile of ashes and say, "Well, he had a good life."

And they would be right. I have survived many adventures in life. I have loved and been loved. I have cried and laughed. I have experienced fear and I have known happiness. If life offered a do-over, I would not change a thing.

As I close out my life, I would like to leave a few words of wisdom to my progeny. Nothing can say it better than a paragraph from the *Song of Minnehaha*.

"When you read this you will know that I am gone. Summer went by too quickly, but you made my last days enjoyable. Please do not cry for me. I am happy now, for I am Minnehaha the waterfall, and I must return to my homeland. I have gone to join my Hiawatha, and together we shall walk along the shores of Gitche Gumee by the shining Big-Sea-Water. If you come to visit, which I hope you do, you will find me in the mournful cry of the loon or the chirp of the cricket or the susurration of the gentle water fall. I will be there for you.

Acknowledgments

This autobiography would not have been possible without the help of a multitude of people.

Arthur Buege: My Grandfather was the best story teller. I only wish I had taken notes. His descriptions of his youth were the motivation behind this biography.

Jack Buege was a partner in my legally-questionable youthful activities. He provided details I had forgotten. He was also helpful in finding errors that my mental autocorrect overlooked.

Elaine Buege found the errors both Jack and I had missed.

My wife Nancy who put up with my long hours on the computer.

Bill Tanner filled in details about the B & T Dairy neither Jack nor I could remember.

John Anderson, a fellow high school classmate, provided details about his schooling at the one-room Buck School.

Fran Ebers Rollert is another classmate who provided similar information about Koon School.

Classmates **Sandy Stevens Frith, Dale Andrus,** and **Kathy Lang** for pointing out errors in the first edition or providing additional content.

Roger Straw and **Steve Brown** were my roommate and suitemate at Michigan State. Despite their anti-war views, they were willing to accept a returning veteran as a friend. They helped me survive.

Jim Lyals, Adele Bradford Jones, and the **Sparta Historical Commission** for providing many of the historical photos.

Merle E. Proctor (1937 – 2019) for her beautiful line drawing on the cover.

The Sparta Township Library Staff, past and present, who fostered my reading and later writing addiction.

No acknowledgment would be complete without mentioning **Allen Jagielo, Craig Yates** and the 58,318 service men and women who did not return from Vietnam. They were instrumental to this narrative. May they rest in peace.